Scenes 4 3 2 10 Players

by Sandy Hill

ten scenes for young performers

Dramatic Lines

DRAMATIC LINES, TWICKENHAM, ENGLAND
text copyright © Sandy Hill 2002
illustrations copyright © Sandy Hill 2002

This book is intended to provide resource material for speech and drama festivals, workshops, examinations and for use in schools and colleges. No permission is required for amateur performance.

No reproduction copy or transmission of any part of this publication may be made without written permission of the publisher.

Application for performance by professional companies should be made to:

Dramatic Lines
PO Box 201
Twickenham
TW2 5RQ
England

A CIP record for this book is available from the British Library

ISBN 0 9537770 8 1

Scenes 4 3 2 1 0 Players first published
in 2002
by
Dramatic Lines
Twickenham England

Printed by The Dramatic Lines Press
Twickenham England

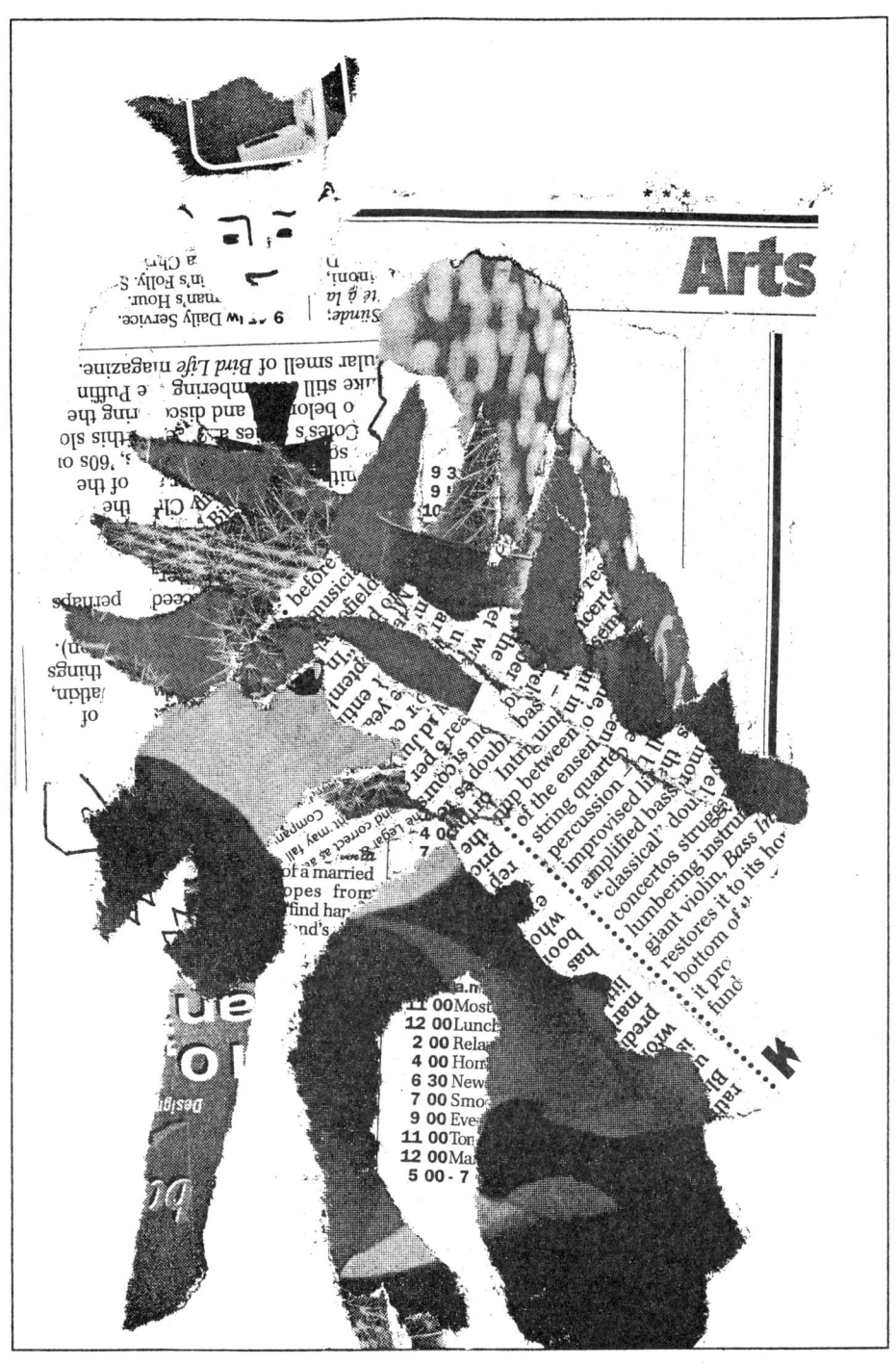

The Art Gallery 1

I dedicate this book to my family and all my pupils past and present and future with whom I enjoy improvising the ideas in embryo form.

Contents

1.	The Death of Deidre Doll	1
2.	The Uninvited Guest	11
3.	Playing God	27
4.	Banbury Ping - a game of?	45
5.	No Way Out - a nightmare	61
6.	The Decision	75
7.	Goldilocks and the Three Burrs	91
8.	Alice and the Mushrooms	101
9.	The Art Gallery	117
10.	Alice in the Wild Wood	135

No of Players Required

The Death of Deidre Doll   3 • 4 PLAYERS
The Uninvited Guest   3 • 4 PLAYERS
Playing God   4 PLAYERS
Banbury Ping - a game of?   4 PLAYERS
No Way Out - a nightmare   5 PLAYERS
The Decision   5 PLAYERS
Goldilocks and the Three Burrs   5 • 6 • 7 PLAYERS
Alice and the Mushrooms   5 • 6 • 7 PLAYERS
The Art Gallery   6 PLAYERS
Alice in the Wild Wood   6 • 7 • 8 • 9 • 10 PLAYERS

Props Costumes and Scenery

Each piece has guidance on props, costumes and sound effects where necessary. These can be freely adapted according to particular circumstances and style of performance.

The Death of Deidre Doll

1. The Death Of Deidre Doll

A GROUP ACTING PIECE FOR THREE GIRLS - AN ADDITIONAL GIRL OR BOY MAY BE INCLUDED.

NOTE : THE USE OF MUSIC IS OPTIONAL THIS PIECE ALSO ADAPTS WELL FOR GROUP MIME WITH MUSIC.

NO OF PLAYERS :   3 GIRLS + 1 GIRL OR BOY *
                                                           * OPTIONAL

CHARACTERS : GIRL ONE
                            GIRL TWO
                            DEIDRE DOLL
                            SAILOR DOLL *
                                       * OPTIONAL

PROPS : 2 OR MORE TRUNKS/BOXES
              A FEW OLD FASHIONED TOYS
              2 OR MORE CLOWNS
              A "BOY" SAILOR DOLL
              STRING FOR CAT'S CRADLE
              TINS (1 CONTAINS A NUMBER OF KEYS)
              A SHOE OR "LIMB"
              A SCREEN (OR FOLDING CLOTHES RACK
              WITH A RUG OVER)
              THREE PARASOLS

COSTUMES : DEIDRE DOLL
                          OLD FASHIONED LACE AND SATIN
                          PRETTY TOP LAYER *

- ELASTICATED WAIST ON SKIRT, WHITE LONG SLEEVED BLOUSE, BOLERO WITH "BUTTONS" AT BACK FOR "PRESSING"

                          UNDERNEATH LAYER - GHOSTLY
                          BLEACHED TORN BURNT VERSION
                          OF TOP LAYER *

THE DEATH OF DEIDRE DOLL

* ADD BURNT CUFFS BEHIND SCREEN

FRIGHTENING GHOST DOLL MASK

<u>GIRL ONE/TWO</u>
PUPPETLIKE RED AND BLUE EYE MASKS,
MATCHING HAIR BANDS WITH WOOLLEN
PLAITS TIED WITH RED AND BLUE RIBBONS *
* *OPTIONAL*

SOUND : LOUD CRASH
        VOICE OF MOTHER
        MUSIC - JAPANESE STYLE, 'AFTER THE BALL',
           'OH YOU BEAUTIFUL DOLL' IN MAJOR
        AND MINOR KEY *
                        * *OPTIONAL*

SCENE : AN ATTIC CONTAINING OLD TOYS. A SCREEN IS STANDING BACK OF THE PERFORMANCE AREA. DEIDRE DOLL IS INVISIBLE TO AUDIENCE SITTING STIFFLY WITH LEGS OUTSTRETCHED IN OR BEHIND A TRUNK OR COVERED WITH CLOTH. GIRL TWO IS HIDING.

[*ENTER* GIRL ONE.]

GIRL ONE : Hello, are you up here? Don't mess about – I can't see a thing. . . . . . Light switch . . . . . light switch. It must be around here somewhere. [SHE SEES GIRL TWO.] What are you doing in here?

GIRL TWO : Just looking around.

GIRL ONE : Mum doesn't like us to come in here.

GIRL TWO : Why not?

THE DEATH OF DEIDRE DOLL

GIRL ONE :   Don't know really.

GIRL TWO :   Look at these old clowns. This one looks as if he's seen a ghost.

GIRL ONE :   You don't think this place is haunted, do you?

GIRL TWO :   Of course not, silly. I was only teasing.

GIRL ONE :   Oh look at this one – could it be Grandma's doll?

GIRL TWO :   [WITHERINGLY.] Grandma's doll was much bigger than that and it was a girl doll. Grandma called her Deidre.

GIRL ONE :   Well I like this boy doll. I shall call him Samuel.

GIRL TWO :   Samuel?

GIRL ONE :   Yes, Samuel.

GIRL TWO :   Oh, oh ..... I know, you're thinking of Sam Hartley, aren't you?

GIRL ONE :   Course not.

GIRL TWO :   Yes, you are. [TEASINGLY.] You fancy him, I know.

GIRL ONE :   This doll's nothing like Sam Hartley. It hasn't got red hair for a start.

GIRL TWO :   Cat's Cradle?

[GIRL TWO TAKES OUT STRING FROM HER POCKET. THEY SIT AND PLAY CAT'S CRADLE

THE DEATH OF DEIDRE DOLL

                                  FOR A MOMENT OR TWO BEFORE IT GOES WRONG. THEY GIVE UP AND GIRL TWO RETURNS STRING TO POCKET.]

GIRL TWO :   I'm so bored.

GIRL ONE :   Me too.

                            [<u>BANG</u> – DEIDRE DOLL'S LEGS CRASH DOWN AND BOTH GIRLS JUMP UP.]

GIRL ONE : ⎱   What was that?
GIRL TWO : ⎰

                            [THEY ARE BOTH SHOCKED AND FRIGHTENED. AFTER RECOVERING THEY SEARCH AND FIND DEIDRE DOLL.]

GIRL ONE : ⎱   Deidre! Grandma's doll!
GIRL TWO : ⎰   Deidre! .... Isn't she old fashioned!

                            [<u>VOICE FROM OFF-STAGE</u> – "GIRLS ..... SUPPER TIME". THEY BOTH TURN TO ANSWER.]

GIRL ONE : ⎱   Coming Mum. .... Just a minute, ...
GIRL TWO : ⎰   Coming Mum. .... We

GIRL ONE : ⎱   .... five minutes, please.
GIRL TWO : ⎰   won't be long, ... okay?

                            [DEIDRE DOLL MOVES WHILST GIRLS ARE ANSWERING MUM. GIRLS TURN TO FIND DEIDRE GONE.]

GIRL ONE :   What have you done with her?

GIRL TWO :   I haven't touched her!

THE DEATH OF DEIDRE DOLL

GIRL ONE :   You must have.

GIRL TWO :   You're so selfish – you just want her for yourself.

                 [GIRLS FIND DEIDRE DOLL LYING DOWN.]

GIRL ONE :   Are you sure you didn't move her?

GIRL TWO :   I promise.

GIRL ONE :   Well it's very weird. She can't just have walked by herself. ..... Can she?

GIRL TWO :   I don't know ..... unless she's some sort of mechanical .....

GIRL ONE :   Help me get her up.

                 [THEY PROP HER UP IN SITTING POSITION.]

GIRL ONE :   She's got little buttons on her back. I wonder ..... [SHE KNEELS ASTRIDE DOLLS LEGS. GIRL TWO PRESSES A BUTTON – DOLL SNAPS ARMS AROUND GIRL ONE.] Get her off – you did that on purpose. Get her off me.

                 [GIRL TWO PRESSES ANOTHER BUTTON. DOLL SNAPS ARMS BACK. GIRL TWO IS KNOCKED OVER AND GIRL ONE FALLS BACKWARDS – DOLL BENDS OVER STIFFLY AT WAIST.]

GIRL ONE :   [PICKING HERSELF UP BEFORE GOING TO PICK UP THE DOLL.] Oh! look ...... look, a keyhole.

THE DEATH OF DEIDRE DOLL

GIRL TWO :   A keyhole? Right; somewhere there must be a key. See what you can find.

GIRL ONE :   [NOTICING SOME TINS. PICKS ONE UP, SHAKES IT, PICKS UP ANOTHER, SHAKES IT - SOUND OF KEYS JANGLING. LOOKS IN TIN.] ..... A tinful of keys. Could be one of these? [TRIES THREE KEYS.] ..... This one fits. [SHE WINDS UP DOLL WHO STRAIGHTENS UP TO SITTING POSITION.]

GIRL ONE :   Help me lift her up.

[THEY LIFT DOLL INTO STANDING POSITION.]

GIRL TWO :   Shall we try a button?

GIRL ONE :   Yes.

GIRL TWO :   Favourite colour?

GIRL ONE :   Blue.

[GIRL TWO PRESSES APPROPRIATE BUTTON ON DOLL'S BACK. DEIDRE DOLL STARTS WALKING WHILST RECITING *MARY, MARY.*]

DEIDRE DOLL :   Mary, Mary quite contrary
How does your garden grow?
With silver bells and cockle shells
And pretty maids all in a row.

[FROM TIME TO TIME THEY TURN DEIDRE DOLL SO THAT SHE DOESN'T BUMP INTO THINGS. WHENEVER SHE IS TURNED SHE SAYS "MARY, MARY, MARY, MARY" UNTIL SHE SETS OFF AGAIN, STARTING THE RHYME FROM THE BEGINNING EVERY TIME.]

GIRL ONE :   Wow - She's quite something isn't she?

THE DEATH OF DEIDRE DOLL

GIRL TWO : I should say – shall we try another one?

GIRL ONE : You chose this time.

GIRL TWO : Okay then ..... brown.

[GIRL TWO PRESSES THE BUTTON – DEIDRE DOLL RECITES *I'M A LITTLE TEA POT* WITH ROUTINE. GIRLS ARE STANDING SO CLOSE TO THE DOLL THAT "THIS IS MY HANDLE" NEARLY KNOCKS ONE OF THEM OVER, AND "THIS IS MY SPOUT" THE OTHER. WHEN THE ROUTINE FINISHES THE DOLL SAGS STIFFLY – THEY FETCH THE KEY AND RE-WIND HER.]

GIRL ONE : Shall I press the brown one again?

GIRL TWO : No. I'm not that keen on "I'm a little tea pot". Try the yellow one.

[THE DOLL MOVES TAKING TINY STEPS ALMOST ON THE SPOT BUT TURNING FIRST TO ONE SIDE AND THEN THE OTHER. HER HANDS ARE TOGETHER PALM TO PALM AND AT THE END OF EACH TURN SHE GIVES A LITTLE FORMAL BOW TO JAPANESE MUSIC.]

GIRL ONE : [CATCHING SIGHT OF THREE PARASOLS LEANING AGAINST A BOX.] Parasols!

[SHE FETCHES THE PARASOLS, GIVES ONE TO GIRL TWO AND PLACES ONE IN DOLL'S HANDS AND KEEPS ONE HERSELF. THE GIRLS ARE ONE EACH SIDE OF THE DOLL AND BOW AS SHE BOWS TO THEM IN TURN UNTIL SHE WINDS DOWN.]

GIRL ONE : I thought she'd go on forever.

GIRL TWO : You could have switched her off.

THE DEATH OF DEIDRE DOLL

GIRL ONE :   I suppose so. Does she need a wind?

GIRL TWO :   Probably. [WINDS DOLL.] What haven't we tried yet?

GIRL ONE: Um ..... green, pink, purple.

GIRL TWO :   Purple, I like purple. Hey, lets try it!

[AFTER PURPLE BUTTON IS PRESSED DEIDRE DOLL STARTS WALTZING TO 'AFTER THE BALL'.]

GIRL ONE : ⎫
GIRL TWO : ⎭   She's waltzing!

[BOTH GIRLS TRY TO COPY HER BUT ARE NOT VERY GOOD. THEY BUMP INTO EACH OTHER.]

GIRL ONE :   I wonder if she'll go faster?

GIRL TWO :   What's that dial? Do you think it would alter the speed?

GIRL ONE :   Dare we try?

GIRL TWO :   Yes.

[THEY TURN UP THE DIAL. THE DOLL WALTZES TO SPEEDED-UP MUSIC. THEY TURN UP DIAL FURTHER. SHE STARTS SPINNING TO EVEN FASTER SPEEDED-UP MUSIC. THEY TRY TO REACH HER TO TURN HER OFF BUT HER ARMS ARE FLARING OUTWARDS. SHE SPINS TO THE BACK AND DISAPPEARS BEHIND THE SCREEN. <u>THERE IS A LOUD BANG</u>. A "LIMB" FLIES OUT AS THE GIRLS WATCH IN HORROR. THEY ARE SHOCKED AND TEARFUL.]

GIRL ONE :   Oh! look what you've done to her!

THE DEATH OF DEIDRE DOLL

GIRL TWO :   [PICKING UP THE LIMB.] She's completely broken.

GIRL ONE :   What will Mum say?

GIRL TWO :   Well don't go blaming me.

[<u>NOTE</u> : ADDITIONAL DIALOGUE /IMPROVISED CONVERSATION MAY BE ADDED TO GIVE DOLL TIME TO TAKE OFF TOP LAYER OF CLOTHING AND TO PUT ON MASK AS BOTH GIRLS STAND WITH BACKS TO AUDIENCE AND PUT ON EYE MASKS AND HAIR BANDS WITH WOOLLEN PLAITS.]

GIRL ONE :   What would Grandma say if she knew?

GIRL TWO :   It's a good thing Grandma can't see what we've done.

[THE GHOST OF DEIDRE DOLL APPEARS FROM BEHIND THE SCREEN TO 'OH YOU BEAUTIFUL DOLL' IN MINOR KEY AND WALKS SLOWLY AND MECHANICALLY TO STAND BETWEEN THE TWO GIRLS. SHE TURNS THEM AROUND ONE AT A TIME TO 'OH YOU BEAUTIFUL DOLL' IN MAJOR KEY. THE GIRLS HAVE BECOME PUPPETS CONTROLLED BY DEIDRE DOLL AND MOVE JERKILY. ALL THREE BOW SIMULTANEOUSLY.]

The Uninvited Guest

2. The Uninvited Guest

NO OF PLAYERS : 3 • 4 GIRLS

CHARACTERS : PARVIA (LATE MIDDLE AGE)
                THROSTINE (LATE MIDDLE AGE)
                MEGAN (YOUNG SCHOOL AGE)
                WOMAN

NOTE : WOMAN] MAY DOUBLE WITH MEGAN

PROPS : 2 CHAIRS AND A TABLE
         RECIPE BOOKS
         PIECE OF PATCHWORK SEWING
         USED ENVELOPE/PAPER SCRAP AND PEN
         TELEPHONE
         BOX OF GROCERIES
         CASSEROLE
         BOTTLE OF RED WINE AND 2 GLASSES

SOUND : DOOR BELL *
                * *OPTIONAL*

SCENE : A KITCHEN ONE SATURDAY AFTERNOON.

          [PARVIA IS LEAFING THROUGH RECIPE BOOKS AND THROSTINE IS SEWING AS USUAL. SHE WORKS DEFTLY WITH HARDLY A GLANCE DOWN - STOPPING AND STARTING UNCONSCIOUSLY AS HABITUAL SEWERS DO.]

PARVIA : [PUTTING DOWN ONE RECIPE BOOK AND CHOOSING ANOTHER.] What shall we have for tonight then?

THROSTINE : [SEWING.] You mean for dinner, dear?

THE UNINVITED GUEST

PARVIA : Yes. Fancy a change, don't you? Something tasty – a casserole perhaps.

THROSTINE : Mmmmm. What about the shopping? I've just settled down with this patchwork for Megan's new cloak.

PARVIA : I'll phone Finchley's. Nigel will deliver, you know.

THROSTINE : Fine, you choose something. I leave it to you, Parvia.

PARVIA : There are some fascinating recipes in this old book of Mildred's. D'you think it's alright to do one?

THROSTINE : I don't see why not. I'm sure she would be very happy to know they were being put to good use. Anything particular in mind, dear?

PARVIA : There's one based on grouse and greengages.

THROSTINE : [SLIGHTLY DOUBTFUL] Mmmmmm.

PARVIA : Or one with partridges, prunes and pecans.

THROSTINE : [MORE DOUBTFUL] Ye . . . . . es.

PARVIA : Or this one . . . . . Oooh, yes, Throstine, listen - ptarmigan, toadstools – edible variety, of course – and tarragon. What do you think of that?

THROSTINE : Well ..... if Finchley's have ptarmigan .....

PARVIA : I'll give them a ring [STANDS AND SHOUTS.] Megan ..... are you in the study? What's Finchley's telephone number?

MEGAN : [FROM OFF-STAGE.] Three-zero, three-zero, three-nine..

THROSTINE : Have you made a list?

PARVIA : Oh no. I'd better hadn't I, before I ring. Lets see ..... [PICKS UP USED ENVELOPE AND PEN THEN SITS DOWN AGAIN WITH RECIPE BOOK AND STARTS TO WRITE THE LIST.] ..... Two ptarmigan.

THROSTINE : Better get four, then there's some for Monday.

PARVIA : [CROSSING OUT.] Four ptarmigan ..... better double the quantity of toadstools; we've got tarragon in the garden. Rice, brown, d'you think?

THROSTINE : Yes ..... brown.

PARVIA : And bacon, bread for breakfast and ..... um ..... do we need more cat food?

THROSTINE : We bought a whole caseful last week.

PARVIA : Well we go through it pretty quickly, now that Bilberry's stopped bringing in mice.

THE UNINVITED GUEST

THROSTINE : And Blackberry hasn't caught a rabbit in months.

PARVIA : Loganberry and Haddock are getting lazy too. Useless creatures, all of them.

THROSTINE : We might need them one day. . . . . . Better get some more Kittycuts.

PARVIA : [SHOUTS.] Megan. Anything else we need from Finchley's?

MEGAN : [FROM OFF-STAGE.] Soap flakes, cat litter, peppercorns and grapefruit marmalade.

PARVIA : We've plenty of ordinary marmalade; won't that do?

MEGAN : [FROM OFF-STAGE.] Uncle Zack's coming for tea and he likes it on his crumpets.

PARVIA : We haven't got any crumpets.

THROSTINE : Add them to the list.

PARVIA : Is that it?

MEGAN : [FROM OFF-STAGE.] Think so.

PARVIA : [DIALS. WAITS TO GET THROUGH.] Hell-o is that Finchley's? . . . . . I'm phoning on behalf of Miss Thistlewick . . . . . I'd like to place an order. Can Nigel deliver this afternoon? . . . . . Before four o'clock . . . . . good, that's fine. Goodbye.

[SHE PUTS PHONE DOWN AND SMILES AT THROSTINE.]

THROSTINE : You didn't give the order, dear.

PARVIA : Didn't I? Silly me. [DIALS AGAIN.] Hell-o. Is that Finchley's? ..... I'm phoning on behalf of Miss Thistlewick. ..... Yes, yes I did. I'm sorry I mean I didn't but I will now give you the order. Four ptarmigan. ..... Are they? ..... Particularly large? Oh well, three then. Edible fungi, ... oh no, I'll need double that quantity at least, ... yes, that's more like it. Two large bags of brown rice, bacon, ... that will be fine, one of those nice granary loaves and a six pack of Kittycuts. ..... a bag of cat litter, ... economy pack, yes please, a large Sudso and a jar of your best grapefruit marmalade and a packet of crumpets. ..... Yes ..... yes ..... on Miss Thistlewick's account. Yes, yes, ... Thank you. ..... Goodbye. [TO THROSTINE.] I'll just get the stove going and find a large casserole. [SHOUTS.] Megan ..... will you get me a big bunch of tarragon from the garden?

MEGAN : [FROM OFF-STAGE.] What does it look like?

PARVIA : Look in the book.

MEGAN : [FROM OFF-STAGE.] Where's the book?

PARVIA : On the back door shelf.

THE UNINVITED GUEST

MEGAN :   [FROM OFF-STAGE.] Right. How do you spell tarragon? Does it start with a P?

PARVIA :   No, silly ..... that's ptarmigan. Tarragon's just like it sounds. T ... A ... double R ... A G O N. ..... Found it?

MEGAN :   [FROM OFF-STAGE.] Ye ... es.

PARVIA :   Good.

THROSTINE :   You forgot peppercorns.

PARVIA :   Did I? Are you sure? [CONSULTING LIST.] ..... They're written down here.

THROSTINE :   Well you didn't say peppercorns.

PARVIA :   Didn't I?

THROSTINE :   No

PARVIA :   I'd better phone again.

THROSTINE :   Unless there are some in the larder. Call Megan.

PARVIA :   She's in the garden.

THROSTINE :   Well, go and see yourself.

               [PARVIA SIGHS AND HEADS FOR LARDER. SHE *EXITS* AS MEGAN *ENTERS* THROUGH FRENCH WINDOWS FROM GARDEN. .]

MEGAN :   [*ENTERING.*] I've brought the tarragon, where's Parvia?

THE UNINVITED GUEST

THROSTINE :   Gone to look for peppercorns.

MEGAN :   I didn't see her in the garden.

THROSTINE :   You wouldn't dear, she's looking in the larder.

MEGAN :   Oh ..... I don't think there are any.

THROSTINE :   No?

MEGAN :   No, Uncle Zack had the last on his Pepper Steak on Friday night.

THROSTINE :   I thought Zack always had fish on Fridays.

MEGAN :   He usually does but Haddock had it.

THROSTINE :   Haddock had it?

MEGAN :   Yes ..... Haddock had the cod Uncle Zack was going to have for supper ..... or was it haddock?

THROSTINE :   You said it was Haddock dear, but it could have been Loganberry.

MEGAN :   No, the cat was Haddock, I'm not sure what the fish was.

THROSTINE :   Oh, I see! He's very greedy, that cat. Time he had some gainful employment.

[*ENTER* PARVIA FROM LARDER.]

PARVIA :   No peppercorns.

THROSTINE :   You'd better ring Finchley's again.

17

THE UNINVITED GUEST

PARVIA : Nigel will have left by now.

THROSTINE : Yes, I suppose so. Are they essential?

PARVIA : What?

THROSTINE : The peppercorns. Are they essential?

PARVIA : Well, I think so ..... the recipe said peppercorns ..... I don't know how I could have forgotten them. ..... Megan will have to go down to the corner shop for some.

THROSTINE : [TO MEGAN.] Yes, Megan, but first wait and give Parvia a hand with the provisions when Nigel arrives.

MEGAN : I was thinking of going out later.

PARVIA : Oh? Where?

MEGAN : Oh, just ..... out.

PARVIA : Well, ... after you've fetched the peppercorns perhaps, but not for too long.

THROSTINE : There are the cats to feed, the table to lay and ..... Have you done your homework?

MEGAN : Some of it.

THROSTINE : How much of it?

MEGAN : Well .....

PARVIA :   Most of it?

MEGAN :   Ummm.

PARVIA :   Half of it?

MEGAN :   Nearly.

THROSTINE :   Doesn't sound as if you should be
              going out at all, does it?

              [MEGAN REMAINS SILENT.]

THROSTINE :   Well, does it dear?

MEGAN :   Just for a little .....

PARVIA :   We'll see.

              [DOOR BELL RINGS.]

THROSTINE :   Ah ..... that'll be Nigel. ..... Go
              and give him a hand, will you dear?

MEGAN :   Alright.

PARVIA :   Cat food in the larder ..... litter in
              the back porch and the rest of the stuff in
              here, please.

MEGAN :   Alright. [*EXITS* TO HALL.]

MEGAN :   [FROM OFF-STAGE.] Thanks Nigel. .....
              Yes there's a lot today ..... and she
              still managed to forget the peppercorns. .....
              Just here please.

              [MEGAN *ENTERS* FROM HALL WITH BOX OF
              GROCERIES.]

THE UNINVITED GUEST

MEGAN : If you want me to get the peppercorns now, Nigel will give me a lift as far as the corner and then I can run back.

PARVIA : Very well ..... here's some change. Don't be long. [MEGAN TAKES THE CHANGE HURRIES BACK TO THE HALL. *EXITS.*] Now, I might as well get this stew going. [LOOKS AT RECIPE.] Says you can use red wine instead of water. ..... What d'you think?

THROSTINE : Well, it is Saturday.

PARVIA : [STARTS ARRANGING FOOD IN CASSEROLE, POURS WINE IN, CHECKS STOVE AND PUTS LID ON. SHE SIGHS.] I'll have to add the peppercorns as soon as Megan brings them.

THROSTINE : Let's hope she's not long. Let's have a drink while we're waiting.

[PARVIA FETCHES GLASSES AND POURS TWO.]

PARVIA : Cheers!

THROSTINE : Santé! Mmmm, very nice. ..... What is it?

PARVIA : Bats blood ..... '61.

THROSTINE : Ah yes, a very good year.

PARVIA : The casserole smells good. I hope Megan doesn't loiter about. It does need the peppercorns to release the flavours.

THE UNINVITED GUEST

THROSTINE : She should have been back by now. Give Finchley's a ring and see how long ago Nigel dropped her off.

PARVIA : [HESITATING.] They'll be sick of me ringing.

THROSTINE : Not at all ..... we're probably their best customers.

PARVIA : I suppose we might be. Hadn't thought of that. [DIALS, GETS THROUGH.] Hell-o, is that um ..... Oh good. This is Miss Parvia Thistlewick. Could I speak to Nigel please? No ..... no ..... nothing wrong with our delivery. ..... I just wanted a quick word. ..... He isn't? ..... What! ..... Hasn't come back at all? Well, yes you must be. ..... So are we our niece is with him, you see. Whatever can have happened?

THROSTINE : [INTERRUPTING.] What's the matter?

PARVIA : [TO THROSTINE.] I'll tell you in a moment. ..... [BACK TO CALL] Yes. ..... No. ..... Yes, ... yes, of course, I'll phone if either of them turns up or if I hear anything. Yes. ..... Yes, ... goodbye for now [REPLACES RECEIVER.] Oh dear.

THROSTINE : What is it?

PARVIA : Nigel never arrived back at the shop. No one's seen him since he set off to bring our order.

THE UNINVITED GUEST

THROSTINE : What on earth are those two playing at? ..... And she knew those peppercorns were urgent!

PARVIA : Zack might arrive any moment now.

THROSTINE : He might have some ideas.

PARVIA : About the casserole?

THROSTINE : About Megan, she is his god-daughter after all.

PARVIA : [LIFTS LID AND SMELLS CASSEROLE.] That's coming along very nicely, peppercorns or no peppercorns.

THROSTINE : Listen!

PARVIA : What?

THROSTINE : I thought I heard something.

PARVIA : Did you?

THROSTINE : I thought I heard someone at the door.

PARVIA : I didn't hear a car. I don't think it can be Zack.

THROSTINE : Look at the cats.

PARVIA : I can't see them.

THROSTINE : No, they're cowering behind the dresser.

PARVIA : Odd!

THE UNINVITED GUEST

[KNOCKING AT THE DOOR.]

PARVIA : There is someone. I'd better go and see. [*EXITS* TO HALL.]

THROSTINE : [LOOKING AROUND FOR THE CATS. SPEAKING TO THEM.] What is it my lovelies? What's troubling you then?

PARVIA : [*ENTERING* FROM HALL.] It's a woman with a large case at the door.

THROSTINE : A suitcase? We haven't invited anyone to stay, have we?

PARVIA : I certainly haven't. [MORE KNOCKING.]

THROSTINE : You'd better let whoever it is in. As long as they're not selling anything.

[PARVIA *EXITS* TO HALL TO FETCH WOMAN. *RE-ENTERS* A STEP BEHIND HER.]

WOMAN : [ENTERING FORCEFULLY.] Is tea ready? I've left my bag in the hall. [TO PARVIA.] You can take it up later. Mmmmm, something smells good [LIFTS LID OF CASSEROLE AND SNIFFS.] . . . . . just a bit short of peppercorns, I think. Zack here yet?

PARVIA : You know Zack?

WOMAN : Of course.

THROSTINE : Well, he's not here yet. [BEWILDERED.] Um . . . . . I don't think we've met before.

THE UNINVITED GUEST

WOMAN: Possibly you've forgotten. [PEERS BEHIND DRESSER.] I see you have still got Blackberry, Bilberry, Loganberry and Haddock. I hope they'll get on with my two.

PARVIA: You've brought two cats with you?

WOMAN: Yes, never travel anywhere without a pair of cats. I haven't had these two for long, mind you, but I'm sure they'll shape up, and they seem very fond of each other.

THROSTINE: You'd better put the kettle on Parvia; we'll have tea as soon as Zack gets here. [TO WOMAN.] Won't you sit down?

WOMAN: Thank you, but I'll take my cloak upstairs first. My room's the first on the right at the top of the stairs, isn't it?

THROSTINE: Well no, that's our niece's room.

PARVIA: Megan's room.

THROSTINE: I'm afraid we don't have a spare room.

WOMAN: That's alright; your niece won't be needing it any longer.

PARVIA: What do you mean?

WOMAN: She's not as she was, you see.

THROSTINE: Where is she? What's happened to her?

THE UNINVITED GUEST

PARVIA :   Do you know? Please tell us. We are
              very worried about her.

WOMAN :   She's been ..... "translated".

              [PARVIA AND THROSTINE FREEZE UNABLE TO
               COMPREHEND.] Oh you mustn't worry.
              I'm in charge now.

PARVIA :   What do you mean "in charge"? This
              is our house.

WOMAN :   Not any more.

THROSTINE :   I beg your pardon?

WOMAN :   Oh, you can both stay here. [PAUSE.]
              As long as you do as I say, I'm sure we'll
              all get along very nicely.

PARVIA :   Just who are you?

WOMAN :   What a lot of questions! Do make the
              tea. We won't wait for Zack. I'll just call
              my cats in from the garden. [SHE MOVES
              OVER TO THE FRENCH WINDOWS. CALLS.]
              Nigel ..... Megan ..... come on kitty,
              kitty, kitties!

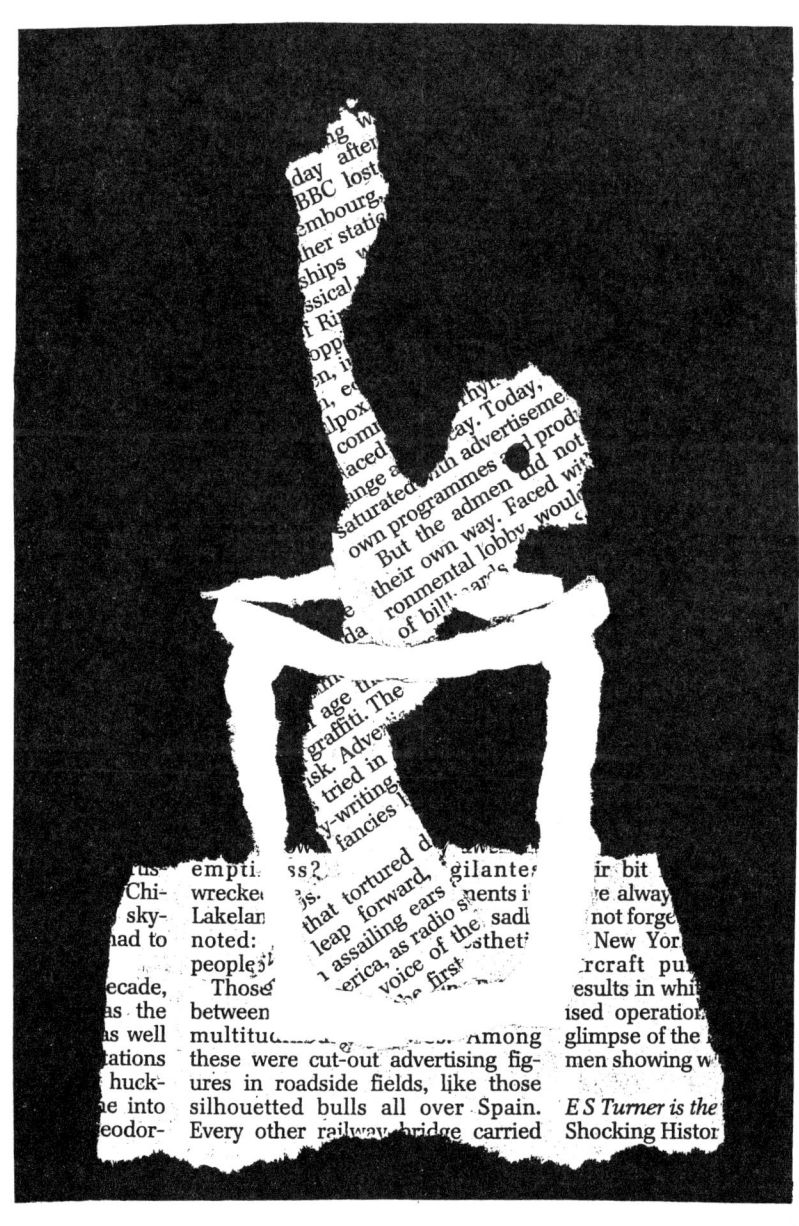

Playing God

3. Playing God

NO OF PLAYERS : 4
                      [GIRLS OR BOYS]

CHARACTERS : HELEN
                    JAY
                    CHRIS
                    PHOEBE

PROPS : LARGE DICTIONARY
            TABLE AND CHAIR
            'BENCH' WORK TOP
            PENCIL AND PAPER
            STACK OF BOOKS
            2 GLASS BEAKERS
            MEASURING JUG
            DROPPER, GLASS ROD, ETC.
            JARS WITH LIDS CONTAINING ITEMS *
            * INCLUDING SMALL 'SKULL'
            SCALPEL-LIKE OBJECT
            MAGNIFYING GLASS
            MATCHES
            LONG HANDLED BRUSH

SOUND : DINNER BELL

SCENE : INSIDE AND OUTSIDE A BIOLOGY LABORATORY AT SCHOOL.

        [HELEN, JAY AND CHRIS ARE HANGING AROUND OUTSIDE THE LAB AT LUNCH-TIME. PHOEBE, AS USUAL, STANDS ALONE A LITTLE WAY AWAY HEAD BURIED IN A DICTIONARY.]

HELEN :   She said create something for Speech Day.

PLAYING GOD

JAY: Did she mean a picture or a model or something?

HELEN: I presume so.

CHRIS: What did she mean by create?

JAY: Ask Phoebe.

[PHOEBE STILL HAS HER HEAD BURIED IN THE BOOK.]

CHRIS: Phoebe, what does create mean?

PHOEBE: Mmmm?

CHRIS: What does create mean?

PHOEBE: Create ..... just a moment ..... [LOOKS IT UP IN THE DICTIONARY AND READS OUT.] ..... Create, bring into existence, ... creating, creation, ...

HELEN: That's given me an idea.

JAY: Good, tell us about it on the way to the studio .....

HELEN: We're not going to the studio .....

CHRIS: But if we have to make something .....

HELEN: It doesn't have to be in the studio .....

JAY: That's where all the materials are though.

HELEN: Not necessarily.

CHRIS: Well, what are you thinking of making?

HELEN :	Do you know the code of the biology lab?
JAY :	The biology lab?
HELEN :	Yes. Do you, Phoebe?
PHOEBE :	Do I? Do I? ..... Sorry, do I what?
CHRIS :	Know the code for the biology lab.
PHOEBE :	I can probably work it out. ..... Why?
HELEN :	We just want to check some work in there – part of a project.
PHOEBE :	Haven't you finished that? It should have been in last Friday.
HELEN :	This is something else.
PHOEBE :	Have you asked Dr. Brown? We're not allowed in there without a member of staff.
HELEN :	I won't touch anything – you come too if you like.
PHOEBE :	All right then. [SHUTS EYES.]
JAY :	Why are you shutting your eyes?
CHRIS :	Ssshh!
PHOEBE :	I'm just trying to remember Dr. Brown's hand movements ..... then I can work it out.
JAY :	You can't, can you?

CHRIS :   She might if you keep quiet.

JAY :   Sorry!

PHOEBE :   [AFTER SOME THOUGHT.] Yes – um
                [USING FINGERS IN THE AIR.] three, three,
                six, five, four – enter. Let me just check.
                . . . . . No, three, three, six, four – enter.
                . . . . . He doesn't actually press five.

HELEN :   Okay. Come on then, before anyone
                sees us. Is the coast clear? [MOVING TO
                LAB DOOR.] Right – I'll do it. Phoebe are
                you coming?

PHOEBE :   You don't need me do you? I was
                thinking of running through my violin solo.

HELEN :   It'd be better if you came – you can
                see we don't do anything silly.

CHRIS :   Yes, please come Phoebe.

                [HELEN ENTERS THE CODE. SHE PAUSES
                BEFORE TRYING THE DOOR.]

JAY :   Hurry up – let's all just get in.

                [THE DOOR OPENS. THEY ALL ENTER
                QUIETLY.]

PHOEBE :   What do you want to check Helen?

HELEN :   Well . . . . . actually I was thinking
                about creating something.

JAY :   You can't create anything in here.

CHRIS :   [TO PHOEBE.] Can she?

PHOEBE : Well theoretically, if we extracted some DNA. . . . . .

JAY : What's DNA?

CHRIS : [TO JAY.] Do you ever listen in lessons?

HELEN : Jay's usually too busy passing notes . . . . . or whispering.

JAY : Am not.

CHRIS : You are.

PHOEBE : Sssh – I'm thinking. [PHOEBE GETS A BOOK OUT AND SITS DOWN AT A TABLE.] Pencil and paper please.

HELEN : [FINDS AND PASSES IT.] Here you are.

[QUITE A PAUSE WHILST PHOEBE WORKS THINGS OUT AND OTHERS TRY AND SEE WHAT SHE IS WRITING]

PHOEBE : Don't all breath on me.

CHRIS : Give her some space.

JAY : You give her some space.

HELEN : Sssh!

CHRIS : Sorry.

JAY : Sorry.

PHOEBE : Shut up!

HELEN : Sorry.

PLAYING GOD

JAY :   Sorry.

CHRIS : Sorry.

PHOEBE : [SIGHS.] ..... Yes ..... I ..... um ..... no, damn! [LOOKS AT BACK OF BOOK.] Ah yes! That's it. Think I've got it. ..... Right. Now then. I'll need ..... [THEY TAKE IT IN TURNS TO FETCH EACH ITEM AS SHE MENTIONS IT.] Glass beaker – um ..... no, two glass beakers. Glass rod, measuring jug ..... dropper ..... matches for the Bunsen burner. ..... Now ..... [SHE WALKS TO THE FRIDGE.] ..... Let's see what's in the fridge. Mmmm ..... [SHE HANDS A JAR TO HELEN.] Take this to the bench - very carefully. [SHE THEN HANDS VARIOUS JARS WITH LIDS TO THE OTHERS BEFORE RETURNING TO THE BENCH. BACK AT THE BENCH SHE STARTS TO MEASURE POWDERS AND LIQUIDS IN TO THE BEAKERS.] Now what sort of things do we want to create – amphibian ..... insect ....

JAY :   Can we chose?

PHOEBE : Theoretically yes – but I'll have to see what's in here that we can extract DNA. from. [SHE LOOKS AT JARS.] Rabbit's feet ..... whole frog ..... Mmmm, not sure what that is – label's smudged. Smells a bit peculiar.

CHRIS : Everything in here smells peculiar.

JAY :   That's putting it politely.

HELEN : [HOLDING UP A JAR.] What's in here?

JAY :	Looks like a knee.
PHOEBE :	No, it's a tiny skull.
CHRIS :	Of what?
PHOEBE :	Or of whom .....
HELEN :	It's a bit small for a whom isn't it?
PHOEBE :	..... Not sure. I'm going to scrape it – pass me something sharp.

[HELEN GOES TO DRAWER AND FISHES ABOUT – PASSES SCALPEL TO PHOEBE. PHOEBE SCRAPES AT THE SKULL AND CAREFULLY TRANSFERS SCRAPINGS INTO ONE OF THE BEAKERS.]

JAY :	What are we making?
HELEN :	Wait and see.
JAY :	What if someone comes?
CHRIS :	Yes, do be quick Phoebe.
PHOEBE :	You can't rush these things.
HELEN :	The bell will be going for lunch soon.
JAY :	No one'll miss us if we don't go.
CHRIS :	They'll miss four of us.
HELEN :	Yes. Why don't you and Jay go?
JAY :	I don't want to go. Why don't you?
HELEN :	I'm helping Phoebe.

PLAYING GOD

CHRIS : We're all helping.

PHOEBE : Sort of ..... pass me that paper.

JAY : This one?

PHOEBE : No! the one with my calculations on, idiot.

CHRIS : [TO JAY.] Idiot.

JAY : Idiot yourself.

HELEN : Sssh! [PASSES CORRECT PAPER.]

[PHOEBE MEASURES LIQUIDS INTO ONE OF THE BEAKERS AND STRIKES A MATCH.]

PHOEBE : Stand back everyone. I'm not exactly sure how volatile some of this stuff is.

HELEN : You're not going to boil it are you?

PHOEBE : Heavens no ..... just bring it to blood heat.

CHRIS : Blood!

PHOEBE : Yes, now who's volunteering?

JAY : Volunteering what?

PHOEBE : To supply the blood.

HELEN : What blood?

PHOEBE : Human blood.

HELEN : Phoebe are you sure you know what you're doing?

PHOEBE : It's quite simple really. I mean . . . . . obviously I haven't tried it before.

JAY : [SARCASTICALLY.] Obviously!

PHOEBE : But theoretically . . . . .

HELEN : Yes?

CHRIS : I'm not giving any blood.

JAY : Well how much do you need?

PHOEBE : Just a drop.

HELEN : Do you have to measure it?

PHOEBE : No I don't think it's critical.

JAY : I've got a scab on my leg I could pick.

CHRIS : Don't be disgusting.

JAY : [TO PHOEBE.] Or I could thump Chris and give her/him a nose bleed.

CHRIS : Don't you dare!

HELEN : We ought to sterilise something sharp and just stab a thumb.

CHRIS : Whose thumb?

PHOEBE : It doesn't matter . . . . . just hurry up and get me a drop of blood.

JAY : Why don't you use your own?

PLAYING GOD

PHOEBE : Listen; do you want me to create something or not?

JAY : If I knew exactly what you were creating.

PHOEBE : It wouldn't be nearly as interesting, would it?

JAY : I suppose not.

[<u>SOUND OF BELL</u> OFF-STAGE.]

CHRIS : Come on, I'm going for lunch. Let's leave her to it. We'll come and see how you're getting on, Phoebe, in half an hour.

HELEN : I'll stay.

PHOEBE : No, go on. Go on it'll be easier if I'm on my own whilst I mix everything.

HELEN : Sure?

PHOEBE : Sure.

HELEN : Okay then. Good luck!

[THEY ALL TROOP OUT, BEING CAREFUL NOT TO BE SEEN LEAVING THE LAB – THEY STOP OUTSIDE LAB DOOR BEFORE HEADING OFF FOR LUNCH.]

JAY : Hope she knows what she's doing.

HELEN : So do I.

CHRIS : Well it was your idea.

JAY :	Yes it was.
HELEN :	Well, I think it was a good idea. Original anyway.
CHRIS :	That's what worries me.
JAY :	How d'you mean?
CHRIS :	Well ..... if it's so original we don't know what to do with it.
HELEN :	We could just sort of leave it somewhere.
JAY :	Where?
HELEN :	The veggie garden or something.
CHRIS :	It might not like veggies.
JAY :	Yeah ..... it might be a carnivore.
CHRIS :	It might eat you all up, Helen.
HELEN :	Oh, don't be silly. It'll probably not develop properly anyway.
JAY :	But it might.
HELEN :	Look, should we go back and tell Phoebe to scrub it?
CHRIS :	Then we've nothing for the Speech Day display.
JAY :	I'd rather have nothing than something that's dangerous
CHRIS :	How could it be dangerous?

PLAYING GOD

HELEN :   I'm going back to the lab. I'm going to stop her.

[HELEN CREEPS INTO THE LAB FOLLOWED BY THE OTHERS. THEY STOP IN THEIR TRACKS. PHOEBE IS HOLDING UP A BEAKER AND SMILING AS SHE LOOKS INTO IT. SHE TURNS AND SIGNALS SSSSH!]

PHOEBE :   [WHISPERING.] Come and look at this.

HELEN :   What?

PHOEBE :   Don't make a noise ..... just come and look.

HELEN :   Oh, wow! What is it?

JAY :   Is it alive?

PHOEBE :   I'm pretty sure it is.

CHRIS :   How can you tell?

PHOEBE :   Look at the middle of the larger shape.

CHRIS :   [POINTING.] There?

PHOEBE :   Yes. Can you see it pulsating?

JAY :   Something going flick, flick, flick under the skin?

HELEN :   Is it skin?

PHOEBE :   Some sort of skin, yes.

CHRIS :   What are those little lumps?

PHOEBE : I'm not sure yet. Is there a magnifying glass somewhere?

HELEN : [SCRABBLES AROUND FINDS ONE.] Mmm. Here's one. [HANDS IT TO PHOEBE.]

PHOEBE : Yes. I thought so. I think they're going to be eyes.

JAY : <u>Eyes</u>?

CHRIS : But there's three of them.

HELEN : Maybe one's a nose.

CHRIS : What about a mouth?

JAY : It hasn't any legs.

HELEN : It might not be going to have any.

PHOEBE : It might have fins, gills. It's a bit too early to say really.

CHRIS : I don't like the look of it.

HELEN : Well, what are we going to do now?

PHOEBE : Wait.

JAY : We can't wait in here long. It'll be registration soon.

HELEN : Well we can't just leave it. Anything might happen.

CHRIS : I wish we hadn't started this. Why don't we just put it in the bin?

PLAYING GOD

PHOEBE : You can't do that ..... it'd be an awful waste. Can someone pass me down that book?

HELEN : Which one?

PHOEBE : Far end of the top shelf.

JAY : This one? [PASSES BOOK.]

PHOEBE : That's the one. [SHE OPENS IT, TURNS A FEW PAGES.]

JAY : What are you looking for?

PHOEBE : Rates of development. Cell division.

HELEN : You've lost me.

JAY : Me, too.

CHRIS : That's not the only thing you've lost [THEY ALL TURN.] Come and see.

HELEN : It's gone!

CHRIS : Exactly.

PHOEBE : Oh hell!

JAY : It can't have gone far.

CHRIS : It didn't have any legs.

JAY : Or wings or anything.

HELEN : Look! [POINTING.]

PHOEBE : What?

HELEN :	There's a sort of ..... slimy trail along the bench.
JAY :	Follow it.
CHRIS :	Be careful.
HELEN :	[STARTLED BY A NOISE.] What's that noise?
PHOEBE :	What noise?
HELEN :	Like a heavy, wheezy sort of breathing.
PHOEBE :	Where's it coming from? [THEY ALL SEARCH EVERYWHERE - EVENTUALLY CHRIS DRAWS THEIR ATTENTION TO SOMETHING UP ON THE CEILING.]
CHRIS :	Look! Up there! [ALL GASP IN HORROR.]
HELEN :	Oh my .....
JAY :	Oh no.
CHRIS :	We've got to kill it.
PHOEBE :	We can't do that.
JAY :	We have to, it's growing bigger and bigger. It could be very dangerous.
Chris :	How do we kill it?
HELEN :	How can we reach it?
CHRIS :	Long handled brush.

PLAYING GOD

PHOEBE : We won't need to ..... it's moved over to the corner, it's slithering down the wall.

JAY : Phoebe, please ..... please kill it.

[THEY ALL WATCH INTENTLY AS IT MAKES ITS WAY DOWN THE WALL.]

PHOEBE : I can't.

CHRIS : You made it.

PHOEBE : Created it.

HELEN : Yes, you created it ..... but it's evil.

PHOEBE : How d'you know.

HELEN : It looks evil.

PHOEBE : We probably look evil to it.

CHRIS : <u>Please</u> Phoebe, before it gets any bigger.

JAY : Or multiplies or something.

[THEY WATCH IT REACH THE FLOOR.]

PHOEBE : [SIGHING.] All right. Pass me the brush.

HELEN : [PASSING THE BRUSH.] Are you going to kill it?

[THEY WATCH IT SLITHER INTO A CORNER.]

PHOEBE : Yes.

[PHOEBE HITS THE CREATURE REPEATEDLY. EVERY TIME SHE HITS IT THE OTHERS GASP.]

JAY : Has it stopped moving?

PHOEBE : [PAUSE.] Yes.

CHRIS : It's dead?

PHOEBE : Go, go, all of you. I'll clear it up.

HELEN : I'm sorry Phoebe. Shall I help you?

PHOEBE : No just go.

[JAY, CHRIS AND HELEN LEAVE THE LAB. *EXIT.*]

ENDING A

[PHOEBE STARTS CLEARING UP THEN REALISES THERE'S SOMETHING BEHIND HER. SHE TURNS SLOWLY AND <u>SCREAMS</u>.]

ENDING B

[PHOEBE PICKS UP THE DEAD CREATURE AND SITS ROCKING IT IN HER ARMS.]

PHOEBE : [WHISPERING.] I'm sorry, I'm sorry, I'm sorry.

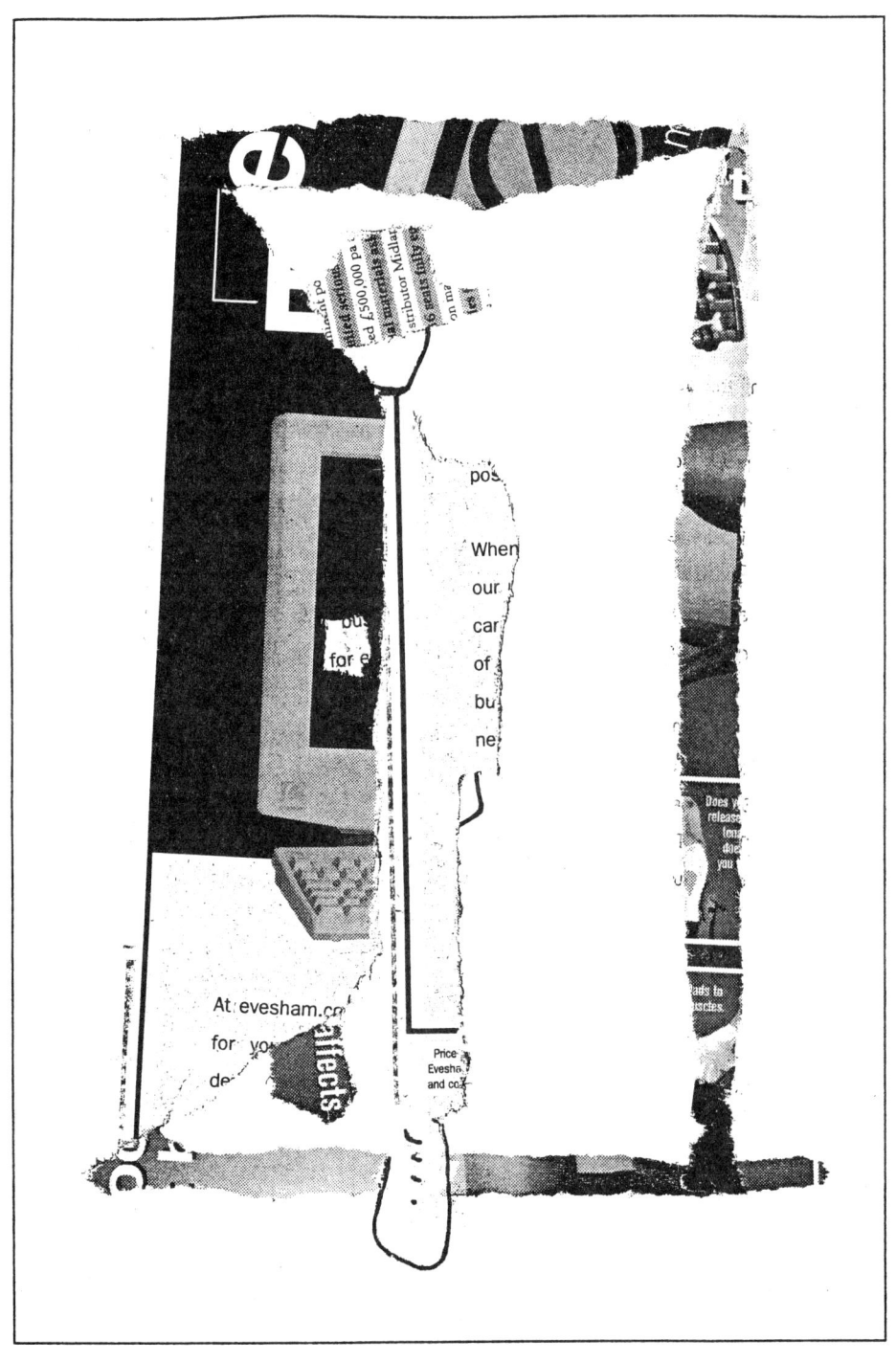

"Come in, come in, wherever you are . . ." Banbury Ping

4. Banbury Ping – a game of..?

NO OF PLAYERS : 4
        [MALE OR FEMALE.]

CHARACTERS : PLAYER ONE
                  PLAYER TWO
                  PLAYER THREE
                  THE STRANGER

PROPS : TABLE AND 4 CHAIRS
          A BOOK
          2 PACKS OF CARDS
          A BUCKET AND SCRUBBING BRUSH
          TRAY WITH FULL JUG AND 4 GLASSES
          CORD OR ROPE
          LARGE SUITCASE FULL OF HATS, SHAWLS,
          PARASOLS, UMBRELLAS, BAGS, ETC.
          3 PADS AND PENCILS, ETC.

          <u>STRANGER</u>
          COAT
          WATCH

SOUND : FOOTSTEPS

SCENE : THE THREE PLAYERS ARE GROUPED AROUND A TABLE.

ONE :   Here we are again, then.

TWO :   Indeed we are.

ONE :   Good game last Tuesday, wasn't it?

BANBURY PING

TWO :   Indeed it was.

ONE :   Very good. Particularly satisfactory ending, didn't you think?

TWO :   Mmmm.

ONE :   I had a feeling though that you ..... [TURNING TO THREE.] ..... felt a little sorry?

THREE : Well ..... perhaps slightly.

ONE :   You know the rules?

THREE : Of course.

ONE :   Well?

THREE : Well what?

ONE :   You know you don't feel sorry for the guests ..... <u>ever</u>. ..... Right?

THREE : Alright, alright.

TWO :   I never allow myself to feel any pity.

ONE :   Quite right ..... once you start on that road you ruin the whole game.

TWO :   Then what's it all been for?!

ONE :   Exactly. [TO THREE.] Don't forget!

THREE : Okay, okay! I'll be tougher!

ONE :   Mind you are then!

TWO :   It isn't as if we use physical violence.

ONE :   No.

TWO :   I suppose we could?

ONE :   Too messy. No, we'll stick to our usual rules. Everyone agreed?

TWO :   Right.

ONE :   [TO THREE.] . . . . . And you?

THREE : Of course. Yes, count me in.

ONE :   Now, it's about five o'clock. There should be one along soon.

TWO :   Hope so.

[PAUSE.]

THREE : Is that someone now?

TWO :   I didn't hear any . . . . .

THREE : [INTERRUPTING.] Listen!

[SOUND OF FOOTSTEPS.]

THREE : Yes, I thought so.

ONE :   All set?

TWO :   Uh-huh!

[THREE NODS.]

BANBURY PING

ONE : ⎫
TWO : ⎬   Come in, come in whoever you are.
THREE : ⎭

ONE : ⎫
TWO : ⎬   Take off your coat. Have a seat.
THREE : ⎭

ONE : ⎫
TWO : ⎬   We've been expecting you.
THREE : ⎭

STRANGER :   [*ENTERING*] Who? Me? Expecting me?

ONE :   Yes, yes, in you come. You're just in time.

STRANGER :   For what?

TWO :   The game of course. Do sit down then we can start.

              [STRANGER TAKES OFF COAT, DRAPES IT OVER THE BACK OF THE CHAIR AND SITS – AND THE GAME BEGINS. THERE IS A RITUALISTIC ROUND OF SIGNS, TAPPING ON THE TABLE, WHICH SEEMS TO MAKE SENSE TO THE THREE BUT COMPLETELY BAFFLES THE STRANGER – HE/SHE MAKES ONE OR TWO FEEBLE ATTEMPTS TO JOIN IN – CAUSING THEM TO SNIGGER OR SHAKE THEIR HEADS.]

STRANGER :   I'm sorry ..... I'm not quite sure what I'm supposed to do.

TWO :   Don't worry old thing, you'll soon pick it up.

ONE :   Most intelligent people do. [TO TWO AND THREE KNOWINGLY.] Don't they?

THREE :   Oh yes, practically always.

TWO :   Oh yes.

STRANGER :   Could you just explain a bit.

ONE :   Not really. [LAUGHS.]

TWO :   Don't think so. [LAUGHS.]

THREE :   Try and watch carefully. Count.

STRANGER :   I'm not sure what I'm supposed to be counting?

ONE :   [LAUGHS.] Oh dear! You always get one don't you!

THREE :   I'm sure you'll pick it up soon.

STRANGER :   Perhaps if I just watched and didn't try to join in?

TWO :   Can't have that I'm afraid, you're signed in until ten o'clock.

STRANGER :   But I never signed anything.

ONE :   But you were signed in. Look there's your name in the book [POINTS TO NAME IN BOOK. That is your name isn't it?

STRANGER :   [LOOKING AT BOOK LONG AND HARD.] Well ..... yes – but I never told you my name. How'd you know who I am?

THREE :   [GENTLY.] You were expected, you know. You mustn't let it worry you.

BANBURY PING

STRANGER : But I don't really know where I am or how I got here.

TWO : Don't you?

STRANGER : No!

ONE : Short term memory loss I expect. Happens sometimes when people are under stress. Are you stressed?

STRANGER : Well I wasn't, but .....

THREE : But?

STRANGER : I think I'm probably getting a bit stressed now.

TWO : Oh that's a shame.

THREE : Yes, you mustn't let yourself get stressed.

ONE : No. It's silly!

TWO : You don't want to be silly do you?

THREE : Do you?

STRANGER : I ..... um .....

ONE : Of course you don't, now, stop worrying. You'll probably do much better in the quiz round.

STRANGER : Is it general knowledge?

TWO : Not exactly.

STRANGER :   Only I'm not very good at general knowledge.

ONE :   [TUT-TUTS.] Tut tut tut!

STRANGER :   Could we play something else?

[ALL THREE LOOK AT THE STRANGER IN AMAZEMENT.]

ONE :
TWO :   You are joking!
THREE :

STRANGER :   Sorry.

ONE :   Alright. But don't let it happen again.

THREE :   Better to do what they say.

STRANGER :   [WEAKLY.] Yes.

ONE :   Pass the cards.

TWO: [PASSES ONE A PACK OF CARDS AND PUTS ANOTHER PACK ON THE TABLE.] There you are.

ONE :   Thank you. [PAUSE.] Right, first question. Who is married to Paul?

THREE :   Philippa.

ONE :   Correct. If you mix yellow and blue, what is the resulting colour?

STRANGER :   [PUTTING HAND UP.] I know . . . . . I know.

BANBURY PING

THREE :   Sh! Not your turn.

TWO :   Green.

ONE :   Very good.

THREE :   [WHISPERING TO STRANGER.] Now it's your turn.

ONE :   What was the answer to three across in yesterday's "Times"?

STRANGER : I don't take the "Times".

ONE :   Wrong. Take a penalty card from the table.

STRANGER : But I do the Daily Mail crossword.

ONE :   Irrelevant. Take two penalty cards.

STRANGER : [TO THREE.] Must I?

THREE :   Simpler if you do.

STRANGER : What do I do with them?

TWO :   Read them of course. Read them out loud.

STRANGER : [TURNS THE FIRST CARD OVER AND READS.] 'Sit under the table for ten minutes.'

TWO :   Come on then.

ONE :   Hurry up [STRANGER SITS UNDER TABLE.] Now, ... the second card.

STRANGER :   I can't reach it.

TWO :   You left it on the table?

ONE :   That was rather stupid. Three?

THREE :   Yes?

ONE :   Pass the card to our dim guest.
[STRANGER'S HAND APPEARS FROM BELOW THE TABLE. THREE PASSES THE CARD.]

TWO :   Read it out!

STRANGER :   Look. Can I go? I um ..... I um .....

THREE :   Don't remember that one.

TWO :   Pass it here. [PUTTING HIS/HER HAND DOWN FOR THE CARD. LOOKS AT CARD.] It doesn't say that at all.

[TWO PASSES CARD TO ONE WHO LOOKS AT IT AND PASSES IT ON TO THREE.]

ONE :   Incorrect reading. <u>Four</u> penalty cards I'm afraid. [HE/SHE PASSES THE CARDS DOWN.] And miss two turns.

STRANGER :   <u>Good.</u>

TWO :   Good?

STRANGER :   [EMERGING FROM UNDERNEATH.] Yes! Good! I don't want any more turns. It was a stupid game.

ONE :   Oh dear, oh dear – a poor loser.

BANBURY PING

THREE : Probably better at manual work.

TWO : I know. Let him/her scrub the floor instead.

THREE : Is that equal to four penalties?

TWO : We'd better check.

ONE : Pass the book. [THREE DOES.] Yes that'll cover it. Two, fetch a bucket and brush.

[TWO DOES – PASSES THEM TO STRANGER.]

ONE : [TO STRANGER.] While you're doing that we'll take a short break. Mustn't get in your way.

STRANGER : But you don't seriously expect me to start scrubbing the floor.

ONE : Certainly we do.

TWO : You can't simply swan in here, join our game and not stick to the rules, you know.

STRANGER : You never even explained the rules.

ONE : If you're going to behave like a spoilt child we'll have to send you to bed.

THREE : Without supper!

STRANGER : [SARCASTICALLY.] I'm really scared!

TWO : Now there's no need to take <u>that</u> attitude.

THREE :	It's not at all helpful.
ONE :	No, it isn't. Now hurry up then we can restart the game.
	[ONE, TWO AND THREE *EXIT* – THEY TAKE STRANGER'S COAT. THREE POPS HEAD BACK AROUND THE DOOR.]
THREE :	It won't take long, and you'll feel a real sense of satisfaction when it's all clean and bright. [HEAD DISAPPEARS.]
STRANGER :	[CHECKS THAT THEY'VE GONE BEFORE TAKING A LOOK AT BOOK ON TABLE. HE/SHE THEN LOOKS AT UNUSED PENALTY CARDS – THE PENALTIES ARE HORRIFIC – HE/SHE GASPS.] I can't do that! . . . . . I couldn't . . . . . Well I'm certainly not playing <u>that</u> game any more. Where's my coat? [CAN'T FIND IT. HE/SHE SEARCHES FOR DOOR – FINDS IT. IT IS LOCKED – HE/SHE BANGS ON IT HARD.] Hey! Hey! Let me out, please. Come on. This is . . . . [LOOKS AT WATCH. PUTS IT TO EAR.] It's stopped! [SHAKES WATCH. HESITATES – GETS BUCKET AND STARTS SCRUBBING. *ENTER* ONE.]
ONE :	[APPEARING BRIEFLY.] Nearly finished? Good. [*EXITS.*]
STRANGER :	I say!
TWO :	[POPPING HEAD AROUND DOOR.] That is going to look very good. [HEAD DISAPPEARS.]
STRANGER :	Just a minute.

BANBURY PING

[THREE *ENTERS.*]

THREE :   Oh, yes – that's really lovely. Oh, that really is marvellous. Well done. Very well done. You must be very proud.

STRANGER :   Well it's only a clean floor.

THREE :   Yes but ..... oh! ..... wait I'll fetch the others. [DOES SO.] Come and look at this. Isn't it magnificent? [ONE AND TWO *ENTER* WITH THREE.]

ONE :   Oh yes. First class.

TWO :   Superb. Where did you learn to scrub a floor like that? I ..... er .... I don't think I've ever seen such a wonderful piece of scrubbing.

THREE :   Professional.

ONE :   Oh, yes. Quite, quite professional.

THREE :   You'll have to have a reward. [TO ONE.] Don't you Think?

TWO :   What does it say in the book?

ONE :   Pass it. [THREE DOES SO AND ONE LEAFS THROUGH – ALL WAIT ANXIOUSLY.] It appears that you can be released with no more penalties.

TWO :   Won't that spoil the game?

THREE :   We'll be short of a player.

ONE: [TO STRANGER.] Would you like to go?

STRANGER: Yes please, if you don't mind.

TWO: Should we let him/her go?

THREE: We'll never find such a floor scrubber again, I shouldn't think.

TWO: [TO STRANGER.] Are you sure you wouldn't like to stay?

THREE: [TO STRANGER.] Just a quick drink before you leave, mmmm?

ONE: It's all quite ready. Why don't you bring it in Three?

[THREE FETCHES A TRAY WITH JUG AND GLASSES.]

TWO: You'll enjoy this.

STRANGER: Well perhaps half a glass. I am a little thirsty after all that scrubbing.

[THREE POURS DRINKS.]

ONE: Cheers. And congratulations on a truly magnificent piece of work.

TWO: Indeed.

THREE: Hear! Hear!

STRANGER: Thank you. Cheers. [SIPS DRINK CAUTIOUSLY – IT IS SURPRISINGLY GOOD AND HE/SHE FINISHES IT.]

BANBURY PING

STRANGER : I'll just sit for a moment before I go, if that's alright. [SITS ON CHAIR AT TABLE – IS FEELING SLEEPY.]

ONE : Yes, why don't you relax for a while. There's no rush is there?

[STRANGER FALLS ASLEEP.]

TWO : Is he/she gone?

THREE : Looks like it.

TWO : How about hanging him/her in the study?

THREE : Is there room for another one in there?

ONE : Well, if not we could always stick one of the old ones up in the attic.

TWO : Good idea.

ONE : Let's make a start then. You know what to do.

[ONE *EXITS*. TWO AND THREE TIE STRANGER TO THE CHAIR WITH CORD – STRANGER REMAINS IN A DEEP SLEEP.]

THREE : Alright? ..... Like that do you think?

TWO : Yes. That's fine [SHOUTS OFF-STAGE TO ONE.] We're ready.

ONE : [*ENTERING* WITH A VERY LARGE SUITCASE]. Here we are.

[THEY RUMMAGE THROUGH SUITCASE FINDING AND DISCARDING HATS, SHAWLS, ETC AND EVENTUALLY DRESS STRANGER UP – ADJUST POSITION OF HEAD, HANDS.]

THREE : How long have we got?

TWO : Before he/she wakes up?

ONE : Forty minutes.

THREE : Can we do it in forty minutes?

ONE : If we get a move on.

[THEY EACH FETCH A CHAIR AND SIT IN A SEMICIRCLE FACING STRANGER. THEN - AT THE SAME MOMENT ALL TAKE OUT/PICK UP PENCILS AND SKETCH PADS AND START DRAWING.]

TWO : Should be a good one.

ONE : Yes.

THREE : Mmmm. Nice ..... very nice.

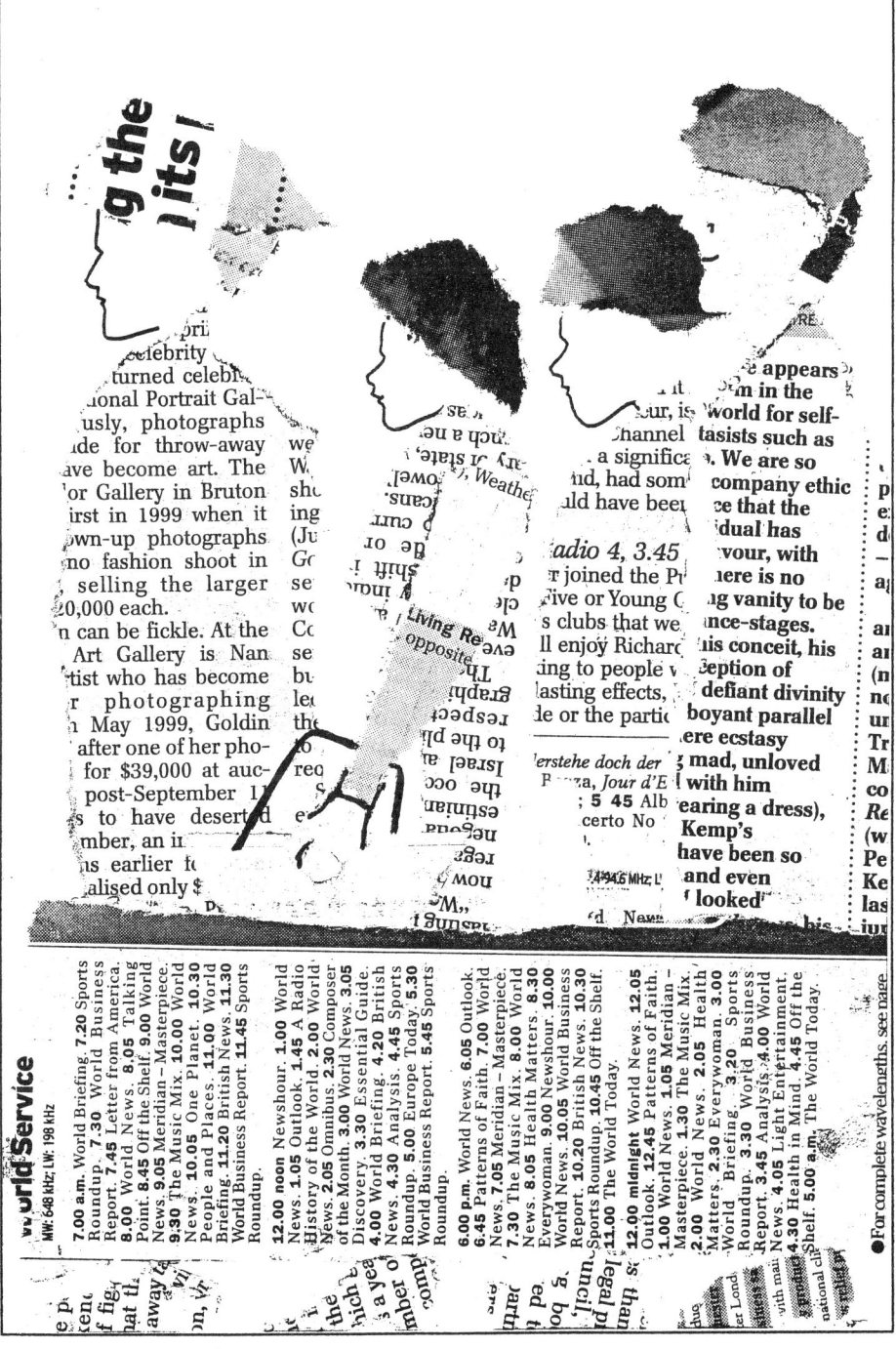

No way Out

5. No Way Out – A Nightmare

NO OF PLAYERS :   5
                 [2 BOYS AND 3 GIRLS]

CHARACTERS :   MRS SYLVIA SHAW
                 HECTOR HARRISON
                 CELIA PEDDING *
                 MARY SMITH
                 JOHN GRAY
                              * NIECE OF PROPRIETOR

PROPS :   SHOPPING LIST
          A SMALL STACK OF SUPERMARKET BASKETS
          SHOPPING ITEMS *
          * INCLUDING MARMITE, CORNFLAKES,
            BLACKCURRANT THROAT PASTILLES, A PACK
            OF 4 BATTERIES, A NEWSPAPER
          NOTES AND COINS
          A TABLE AND CHAIRS
          COFFEE POT, CUPS AND SAUCERS, ETC.
          A MOBILE PHONE.

SCENE :   A SMALL VILLAGE SHOP FIRST THING ONE
          MORNING.

                [SYLVIA WAITS IMPATIENTLY AT THE
                SHOP DOOR WITH SHOPPING LIST IN HAND.]

SYLVIA :   [LOOKING AT WATCH.] C'mon . . . . . c'mon.

                [*ENTER* HECTOR.]

HECTOR :   [ARRIVING.] Morning, aren't they open yet?

NO WAY OUT

SYLVIA :   No, they should be. Maddening, I only want a few things.

HECTOR :   Mmm ..... me too. Wife forgot a few bits and pieces when she did her supermarket trip yesterday.

SYLVIA :   I'm afraid I don't use Peddings much nowadays. They were handy when they used to deliver of course.

HECTOR :   [SURPRISED.] When was that?

SYLVIA :   Oh several years ago now: when they had all that trouble with their nephew.

HECTOR :   Oh I don't think I .....

CELIA :   [OPENING UP.] Good morning. Welcome to Peddings newly refitted handy village store. In you come then .. ...

HECTOR :   [TO SYLVIA] After you.

SYLVIA :   Thank you. [PICKS UP A BASKET – SCANS SHOPPING LIST.]

HECTOR :   [TALKING TO HIMSELF – TUCKING ITEMS INTO HIS HANDS AND ARMS.] Large or small Marmite? ..... Cornflakes ..... Now, what have I forgotten?

CELIA :   Baskets by the door! Please use a basket to make your shopping easier!

HECTOR :   [LOOKING AROUND.] Oh ..... er ..... um ..... right. ..... [DUMPS HIS SHOPPING IN A BASKET.]

NO WAY OUT

[*ENTER* MARY.]

MARY: [BREEZING IN.] Morning Hector. How's Hilary?

HECTOR: Mary. ..... Oh hello. ..... She's fine, ... just sent me down for a few things she forgot. We've got the family staying for the weekend.

MARY: Jolly good. I say they've smartened up in here, haven't they?

HECTOR: A total refit, apparently.

CELIA: [TO MARY.] Baskets by the door! Please use a basket to make your shopping easier.

MARY: Oh, yes ..... right, [PICKING UP A BASKET.] jolly good!

SYLVIA: Morning Mary. Jim better?

MARY: Yes. Thank you. It was only a cold – but you know what men are like with a cold or a headache: think they're dying.

SYLVIA: Mmmm. That reminds me - blackcurrant pastilles: Jack's got a bit of a throat.

[*ENTER* JOHN WITHOUT TAKING A BASKET.]

JOHN: Morning Celia, I see you've had a make-over.

CELIA: Pardon?

JOHN: Shop. Very smart.

NO WAY OUT

CELIA : Ah yes, we aim to please ..... move with the times. Baskets by the door! Please use a basket to make your shopping easier.

JOHN : [TO SYLVIA.] 'Scuse me. Sorry ..... can I just um?

SYLVIA : Sorry, am I in the way?

JOHN : No, no, I can get past now. Only want a thing or two.

CELIA : [LEANING OUT FROM CHECKOUT.] Baskets by the door. Please take a basket.

[SYLVIA AND HECTOR HAVE REACHED THE CHECKOUT BUT CELIA HAS LEFT IT TO APPROACH JOHN WITH A BASKET.]

CELIA : [OFFERING THE BASKET.] Please take a basket.

JOHN : Well, I don't really need .....

CELIA : To make your shopping easier.

JOHN : But ..... [TAKING THE BASKET.] Oh well, thank you.

CELIA : We aim to please. [BROAD SMILE – SHE SCURRIES BACK TO CHECK OUT.] Sorry to keep you waiting. [CHECKS HECTOR'S THINGS THROUGH. HE HAS TEN ITEMS].] Ah .....

HECTOR : Is there a problem?

NO WAY OUT

CELIA: You have more than eight items.

HECTOR: I thought I could have ten.

CELIA: Sorry: more than eight items should go through the regular check out.

HECTOR: [SIGHING.] Well, I'll take them to the regular check out then. [TO SYLVIA.] Sorry about this.

CELIA: I'm afraid I'll have to check the eight items through here: they're already in the system, you see.

HECTOR: Oh really! Surely you can just . . . . .

CELIA: I am sorry . . . . . If it were up to me . . . . . Rules are rules. You can pay for these and join the queue again. I'm sure it won't take long.

SYLVIA: Can I help? I'll get them for you and you can settle with me afterwards.

HECTOR: Are you sure? . . . . . I am in a bit of a rush actually . . . . . that would be a great help.

SYLVIA: Absolutely fine. I've only got five of my own.

HECTOR: [TO CELIA.] Right, I'll settle for these. Mrs Shaw will pay for the batteries and the bread.

CELIA: It's very irregular.

SYLVIA: No problem, surely?

NO WAY OUT

CELIA: Well I don't know. I may have to check with my Uncle.

JOHN: Sorry to butt in, but I am in rather a hurry – can I just pay for this paper?

CELIA: Have you got the correct change?

JOHN: Um, yes. Here it is.

CELIA: Er, no. You're a penny short.

JOHN: Oh sorry – well, I've got a pound here.

MARY: Let me give you the penny ..... then we can all get on.

CELIA: I don't know what Uncle will say. Everyone paying for everyone else's shopping. Just when I've got my new system up and running.

MARY: It won't interfere with your new system dear. [MARY HANDS CELIA THE EXTRA PENNY.]

JOHN: [TO MARY.] That's awfully good of you.

MARY: Not at all. Only too glad to help. [JOHN TAKES NEWSPAPER AND HEADS TOWARDS WHERE HE THINKS THE DOOR IS. IT ISN'T THERE – HE SEARCHES IN VAIN AND RETURNS TO QUEUE.]

JOHN: [TO SYLVIA.] I say, I do feel a bit of a fool but ..... um, since the alterations ..... um ..... I can't seem to find the door.

SYLVIA: Just along from the shampoo ..... I think.

JOHN :   No, that one seems to lead to the back of the shop . . . . .

SYLVIA :   That's funny. Just a moment . . . . .

              [MEANWHILE HECTOR PAYS FOR HIS EIGHT ITEMS.]

HECTOR :   There . . . . .

CELIA :   Thank you . . . . . and one pound and a penny change. Thank you. Do call again.

              [HECTOR MOVES FROM THE CHECKOUT.]

SYLVIA :   There are five of my items, could you give me a subtotal? And the batteries and bread for Mr Harrison.

CELIA :   I can do the bread and two of the batteries.

SYLVIA :   What?

CELIA :   Or three of the batteries and no bread.

SYLVIA :   But it's one pack of batteries.

CELIA :   Yes, but the cellophane's torn you see. So there are now four individual batteries.

SYLVIA :   [GETTING CROSS.] This is ridiculous.

HECTOR :   What's the trouble now?

SYLVIA :   Apparently the batteries are separate items so now I've got too many things for this check out.

NO WAY OUT

HECTOR: Gosh; I'm sorry. If I'd known. Just get your own things, Sylvia. I don't think I'll be coming here again in a hurry.

CELIA: [TO SYLVIA.] Is it just five items now, dear? Do make up your mind. People are waiting you know!

SYLVIA: [THROUGH GRITTED TEETH.] Just the five. Here. [HANDS OVER THE MONEY.]

CELIA: Anything smaller?

SYLVIA: No.

CELIA: Just excuse me then. I have to get some more change. [SLIDES OUT OF CHECKOUT.]

SYLVIA: [TO HECTOR.] I'm not coming here again either. [TO JOHN.] John, have you found the door yet?

JOHN: No, I haven't. It has to be here somewhere. I mean, we all came in by it, didn't we?

MARY: [EMERGING FROM BEHIND SOME SHELVES.] You're going to think I'm a real idiot, but I can't seem to find my way out.

HECTOR: John can't either. Just a minute. I'll have a look. [HE DOES AND RETURNS.] That's very odd [TO MARY.] Have you done your shopping then?

[CELIA RETURNS AND GIVES SYLVIA HER CHANGE.]

NO WAY OUT

MARY: [TO HECTOR.] No. I decided I couldn't stand the excitement!

[HECTOR AND MARY LOOK FOR THE DOOR AGAIN.]

SYLVIA: [TO MARY.] Very wise. [TO CELIA.] Have you changed the door position? It looked the same from outside, but we can't seem to find our way out.

CELIA: There isn't one.

SYLVIA: Sorry?

CELIA: No need to apologise.

SYLVIA: I'm not apologising. I'm asking where the door is.

CELIA: Which one?

SYLVIA: The one to get out. Or the one where we came in for that matter.

JOHN: Presumably the same thing.

CELIA: Ah now, that's where you're wrong.

[HECTOR AND MARY RETURN.]

HECTOR: [TO MARY.] I'm sorry. [TO CELIA] You're going to have to show us the way out.

MARY: It's all ..... different.

JOHN: Well, they've rearranged things yes but .....

NO WAY OUT

MARY : No ..... really different. Different from when I arrived twenty minutes ago.

SYLVIA : Surely not.

MARY : There's a coffee shop.

JOHN : A coffee shop?

CELIA : Whoops! Is that ten thirty already. Time to serve coffee.

SYLVIA : I'm not staying for coffee. Jack'll wonder where on earth I've got to as it is.

JOHN : Yes, I must dash. If I could just find the bloomin' way out. [TO CELIA] If you could just show me the door ..... please.

CELIA : Not at the moment, I'm afraid. Coffee to serve you see. Do excuse me, won't you?

HECTOR : Look here, Miss Pedding, as far as I know, none of us here requires coffee, but we all wish to leave the shop. Now.

CELIA : Dear me. You can't leave without coffee. I'm sure the ladies would like a cup, wouldn't they?

MARY : I think I ought to be going home, if you don't mind.

SYLVIA : I'm certainly not staying.

CELIA : It's really good coffee. I know you'll enjoy it.

NO WAY OUT

HECTOR: The door, please, Miss Pedding.

CELIA: All in good time, Mr Harrison. [TO ALL.] Do take a seat won't you?

SYLVIA: This is absolutely ridiculous. [TO HECTOR.] Can't you make her show us the way out?

[THEY EDGE AWAY FROM CELIA IN ORDER TO TALK TOGETHER FREELY.]

HECTOR: I'm not sure how. She doesn't seem to respond to reason.

SYLVIA: I've always thought her very strange.

JOHN: It's not just her that's strange. I mean how can a door disappear?

HECTOR: It can't. Can it?

MARY: But it has. It's ..... nowhere.

SYLVIA: It has to be somewhere. Perhaps if we all look.

[SYLVIA, HECTOR, MARY AND JOHN SEARCH FOR DOOR. CELIA MOVES OVER TO THE COFFEE SHOP TABLE. THEY SEARCH IN VAIN AND FINISH UP AT TABLE WHERE THEY ARE FACED BY CELIA WITH A COFFEE POT – THEY FIND THEMSELVES RELUCTANTLY SITTING DOWN ONE BY ONE.]

CELIA: That's right, make yourselves comfortable. Milk and sugar on the table. [SHE POURS COFFEE AND THEN MELTS AWAY.]

SYLVIA: I really don't know why I'm sitting here.

NO WAY OUT

HECTOR : Me neither.

MARY : It's rather good coffee, actually.

JOHN : That's as maybe, but I really must go.

MARY : Maybe she'll show us the way out when we've finished our coffee.

HECTOR : She'd better.

CELIA : [REAPPEARING.] More coffee anyone?

SYLVIA :
HECTOR :
MARY :
JOHN :
} No thank you.

CELIA : No charge for a refill you know.

JOHN : You mean you're charging us for the coffee?

CELIA : Only for the first cup, and it's very reasonable.

SYLVIA : I don't see why we should pay anything at all. We didn't want coffee in the first place.

CELIA : But you've all enjoyed it, haven't you?

MARY : Well . . . . .

CELIA : Of course you have.

MARY : Well how much is it?

CELIA : That depends.

NO WAY OUT

HECTOR: On what?

CELIA: Aha!

HECTOR: Enough. [RISING.] There's ten pounds. That should more than cover it for all of us, I think. Now, the door please. Now!

[THEY ALL RISE AND STAND BACK FROM THE TABLE.]

CELIA: [CELIA SMILES TO HERSELF.] Can none of you find it?

JOHN: We don't seem to be able to, no.

CELIA: Do you know why that is?

JOHN: I'm sure you're going to tell us.

CELIA: Do you want me to?

JOHN: Please.

CELIA: It's because ..... there isn't one. [LAUGHS.]

MARY: Look dear. We all came in through a door, so there has to be one somewhere.

CELIA: There was.

SYLVIA: How do you mean was?

HECTOR: The girl's plainly not normal.

CELIA: There was a way in for a while, but there's no way out: never was.

NO WAY OUT

MARY: Well can we go out the in, if you know what I mean?

CELIA: I'm afraid that's out of the question.

HECTOR: Why is it out of the question?

CELIA: He wouldn't like it.

HECTOR: Who wouldn't like it?

CELIA: Uncle wouldn't like it.

JOHN: D'you think we could just have a word with your Uncle, perhaps?

CELIA: No, he doesn't see anyone personally, nowadays. He's very busy, is Uncle Lucy.

MARY: Lucy? That's a funny name for an Uncle.

CELIA: Well it's short for Lucifer, you see.

[THEY ALL LOOK ALARMED AND SIT DOWN AT THE TABLE AGAIN.. HECTOR GETS OUT A MOBILE PHONE – BUT CAN'T GET IT TO WORK.]

CELIA: It won't work down here, I'm afraid.

SYLVIA: Down where?

CELIA: Don't you know? [LAUGHS.] More coffee anyone?

[OTHERS ALL LOOK AT EACH OTHER IN HORROR.]

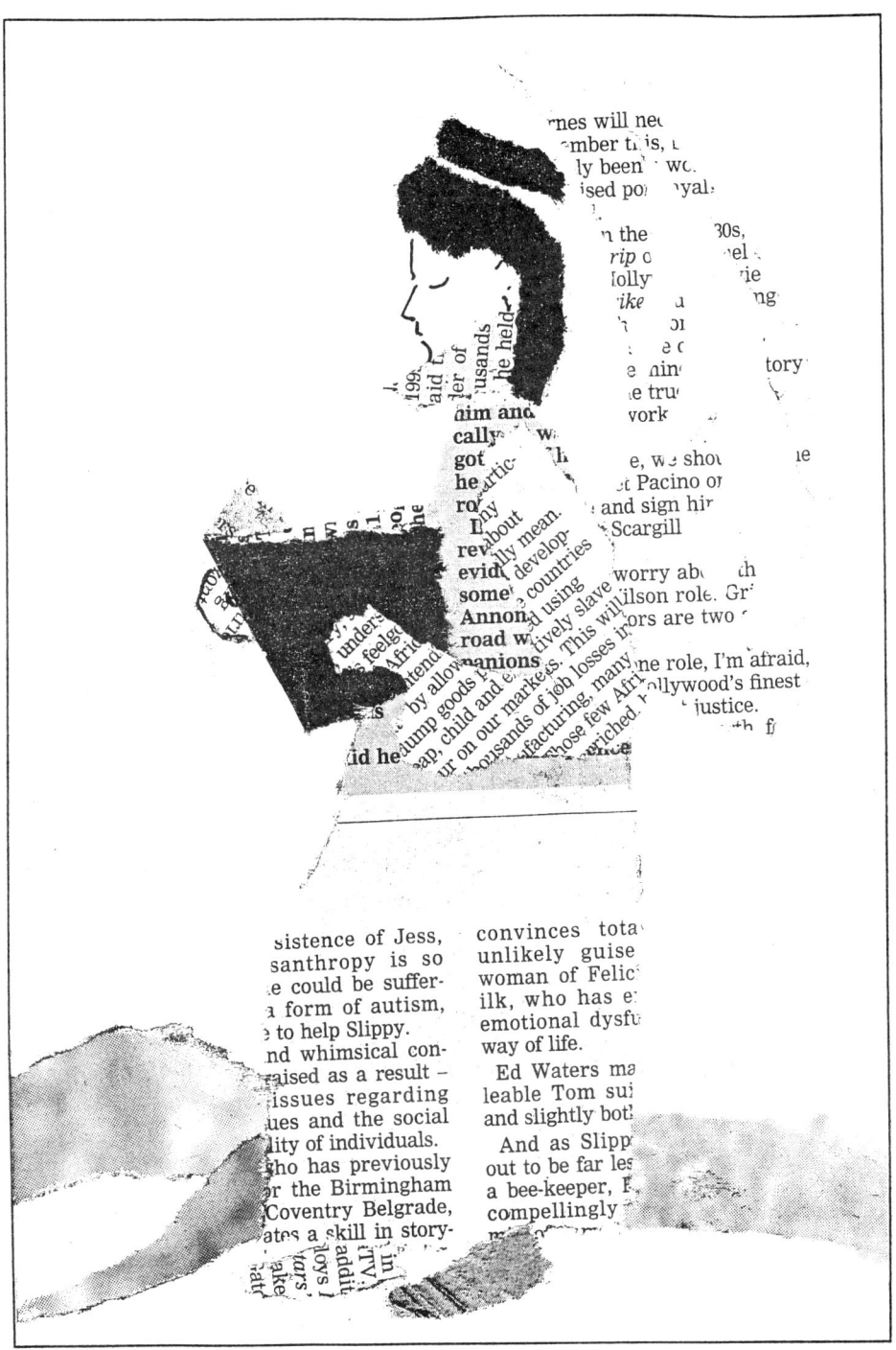

The Decision

6. The Decision

NO OF PLAYERS : 5
 [3 GIRLS + 2 BOYS
 4 GIRLS + 1 BOY
 5 ALL GIRLS]

CHARACTERS : CHLOE (A TEENAGER)
 KATE (A TEENAGER)
 MANDY (A TEENAGER)
 ANGEL *
 ST PETER *

 * HAVE CHARISMATIC PEACEFUL ETHEREAL QUALITIES

PROPS : FILES OF PAPERS
 TABLE AND 1/2 CHAIRS

COSTUMES : <u>ANGEL</u>
 FASHIONABLE CASUAL WEAR POSSIBLY SINGLE COLOUR AND NOT THE TRADITIONAL CONCEPT

 <u>ST PETER</u>
 FORMAL SUIT OR LONG FLOWING COAT

SCENE : CHLOE, KATE AND MANDY ARE QUEUING AT THE THRESHOLD OF A BEAUTIFUL PLACE. MANDY IS ASLEEP ON HER FEET. ST PETER IS A FROZEN STATUE SITTING BEHIND A TABLE TO ONE SIDE OF THE PERFORMANCE AREA.

 <u>NOTE</u>: AT FIRST WE DO NOT KNOW THIS PLACE IS HEAVEN.]

CHLOE : [PUZZLED.] ..... Where? .....

THE DECISION

KATE: This is nice ..... didn't think it would be like this. Where are Nicky and Jo?

CHLOE: Haven't seen them. Is there a queue to get in?

KATE: We already are in ..... I think .... it's much warmer than the other place.

MANDY: [WAKING.] Which other place?

KATE: The place we visited yesterday.

MANDY: Oh ..... yes ..... I'm sure I was carrying my packed lunch. Have you got yours, Chloe?

CHLOE: No. I ..... I ..... haven't got my jacket, either.

KATE: Nor me. ..... We must have left everything behind on the bus.

CHLOE: Where is the bus? I don't remember getting off.

MANDY: I don't. I don't remember anything since ..... since we were speeding down that mountain road.

[*ENTER* ANGEL CARRYING SEVERAL FILES OF PAPERS.]

ANGEL: Hello there. Sorry you're having quite a wait. We've had a particularly large intake today.

MANDY: Sorry.

THE DECISION

ANGEL: Don't worry ..... we don't mind being busy. Rather enjoy it, in fact.

KATE: Have we come to the wrong gate? We seem to have got separated from the rest of our party.

ANGEL: Well yes, you will have done. You're the three from the bus aren't you? [LOOKS AT PAPERS IN FILE.] And I see there's a fourth one of you due tomorrow.

CHLOE: There are twenty-nine of us in our party – where are the others?

ANGEL: Oh dear! Don't you remember what happened? Someone will explain everything to you, soon. Don't worry. I'll see you later. *[EXITS.]*

MANDY: What on earth was he talking about?

CHLOE: Heaven knows.

KATE: What did he mean about tomorrow?

CHLOE: Honestly haven't a clue.

KATE: Well, I'm going to have a wander – keep my place for me.

MANDY: Okay.

[EXIT KATE.]

CHLOE: Hope she'll find her way back before we get to the front of the queue.

MANDY: What exactly are we queuing for?

77

THE DECISION

CHLOE :   Not sure.

MANDY :   I wish I knew where the others were. Jane's got my Walkman.

CHLOE :   You won't need it here.

MANDY :   Why won't I?

CHLOE :   There's music here already.

MANDY :   Is there?

CHLOE :   Can't you hear it?

MANDY :   I don't think so ..... but ..... I can kind of feel it.

CHLOE :   How d'you mean?

MANDY :   Don't know. ..... I just ..... Do you feel kind of different?

CHLOE :   Different to what?

MANDY :   Different from yesterday ..... different from this morning.

CHLOE :   I haven't thought about it.

MANDY :   [STARING AT CHLOE.] You look different.

CHLOE :   Do I? How different?

MANDY :   Um ..... paler.

CHLOE :   You do, too.

MANDY :   Something's very strange.

THE DECISION

CHLOE: Maybe it's the light here. Everything's very bright, isn't it?

MANDY: It's a beautiful place.

CHLOE: Are we getting any nearer the gate?

MANDY: Do you think the others are in, already?

CHLOE: That chap said he'd explain.

MANDY: Yes but he's disappeared.

CHLOE: So's Kate.

MANDY: Bet she's got lost.

MANDY: Maybe she's found Nicky, Jane and Jo.

[*ENTER* ANGEL]

ANGEL: Won't be long now. Where's your friend?

MANDY: You mean Kate?

ANGEL: [LOOKING AT NOTES.] Er, yes ..... Kate.

CHLOE: She went to have a look around.

ANGEL: Ah. [SIGHING.] ..... she shouldn't be wandering around. Not before she's been given her ..... um ..... her [SMILES.] seal of approval.

CHLOE: How'd you mean?

ANGEL: All will be revealed ..... in time.

THE DECISION

[*ENTER* KATE.]

KATE : [RUSHING IN.] Are you still waiting? I say it's the most fantastic ..... most amazing place. : ..... gardens, peacocks .... just fantastic ..... beautiful ..... all sorts of awesome things : and I met this lovely old lady ..... spitting image of Mum's Auntie Grace ..... she was reading stories to a group of small children.

MANDY : Well! .....

KATE : And she said how lovely it was to see me ..... to see me again. It was really odd.

MANDY : Gosh!

ANGEL : We told her you were coming ..... she's been so excited, dear thing.

CHLOE : Kate ..... didn't your Auntie Grace die last year?

KATE : Yes she did. This obviously wasn't her, but it was so like her.

CHLOE : But ..... if this lady was thrilled to see you?

MANDY : [STARING AT ANGEL.] Where exactly are we? Please tell us.

ANGEL : Just be patient : you'll be signed in soon and everything will become clear.

MANDY : Where are the others though?

ANGEL: I had better explain; sit down a moment : you don't remember anything about the start of your journey?

KATE: You mean to the park? We were all on a coach; I was next to Nicky and .... no I can't seem to remember anything else.

ANGEL: Your coach ran out of control on a mountain road ..... it went over the edge .....

CHLOE: But ..... we seem to be alright.

MANDY: What about the others?

CHLOE: Are the others hurt?

ANGEL: Most of them are I'm afraid : Michelle very badly; she'll arrive tomorrow.

MANDY: Will she be okay to travel?

ANGEL: We'll send someone for her. In fact her escort's waiting beside her right now. Is she a special friend of yours?

MANDY: She's my sister.

ANGEL: Ah! [LOOKS AT NOTES.] Yes. That's not so good for your parents is it?

MANDY: I don't understand what you mean.

ANGEL: Losing you both.

MANDY: Losing us?

THE DECISION

ANGEL: They will follow, in forty years or so .....
[A FLEETING SMILE.] of course the time will pass quickly.

[LONG PAUSE. THE THREE GIRLS ALL LOOK AT EACH OTHER.]

CHLOE: } Are we ..... ?
MANDY: }   Is this ..... ?
KATE: } Is it? ..... Is it .....?

ANGEL: Heaven? What do you think? ..... What do you believe?

KATE: Was it really Auntie Grace I saw?

ANGEL: It was.

KATE: So this is heaven?

CHLOE: Wow!

MANDY: We're all dead?!

ANGEL: As far as the earthly life is concerned.

MANDY: But Michelle ..... Can't she stay on earth?

ANGEL: Wouldn't you like her here with you?

MANDY: Yes ..... but ..... Mum and Dad .....

ANGEL: [LOOKING AT NOTES.] She's on tomorrow's list. It's really not up to me : an escort's already been sent, you see.

MANDY: Can't you do something?

THE DECISION

ANGEL: She's very badly hurt : I think she'd be happier here now - totally healed again.

KATE: You can't let this happen; their parents will be distraught.

CHLOE: Hey! What about our parents?

KATE: Oh gosh! poor Mum.

ANGEL: Try not to dwell on it too much. ..... If they believe they will be comforted.

MANDY: But Michelle ..... please.

ANGEL: I'll have to have a word with a higher authority. If she's already in Peter's book it's going to be rather difficult.

MANDY: Please.

ANGEL: [SIGHING.] We'll see what Peter says.

[HE LEADS THEM TO A TABLE. ST PETER IS SITTING BEHIND IT. HE 'COMES TO LIFE' ON THEIR APPROACH AND OPENS A FILE.]

ST PETER: Hello, are you three together?

[THEY NOD - VERY MUCH IN AWE.]

ST PETER: Good journey? ..... I don't expect you remember much about it do you?

[THEY SHAKE THEIR HEADS.]

ST PETER: No, well, let's see. Um .....
[CONSULTING A LIST.] Kate, Chloe and Michelle isn't it?

THE DECISION

MANDY :   Well . . . . .

KATE :   We are, she's not.

ST PETER :   She's not what?

CHLOE :   Michelle . . . . . she's not Michelle.

[ST PETER LOOKS STERNLY AT ANGEL.]

ST PETER :   Can you explain this confusion?

ANGEL :   Yes, Peter; this is Mandy, Michelle's twin sister; Michelle is due tomorrow.

ST PETER :   Well, on my list I have Kate, Chloe and Michelle. Mandy's name has been crossed out.

[ANGEL LOOKS UPWARDS ENQUIRINGLY – ST PETER NODS.]

ST PETER :   Yes. The parents were so distressed, our Father decided to leave her. [TO ANGEL] Didn't you get the message? [PAUSE. ANGEL SHAKES HEAD.] But you should have waited for Michelle: a beautiful dancer, gifted . . . . . but her earthly legs are so badly damaged I think she'd prefer to be here.

MANDY :   You mean I shouldn't be here at all!?

ST PETER :   Not for another seventy-one years.

KATE :   Can you send her back?

ANGEL :   Too late now. I am sorry.

THE DECISION

ST PETER :   [TO GIRLS.] Would you like to wait in the Secluded Rose Garden whilst we try to sort this out? We'll try not to keep you waiting too long.

[ANGEL POINTS OUT THE WAY TO GARDEN. *EXIT* GIRLS. ST PETER AND ANGEL FREEZE AS THE GIRLS *RE-ENTER.*]

CHLOE :   Do you want to go back?

KATE :   He said it was too late . . . . .

[GIRLS FREEZE AS ST PETER AND ANGEL MIME THEIR DISCUSSION. THEY FREEZE IN TURN AND THE GIRLS UNFREEZE.]

MANDY :   . . . . . I kind of like it here . . . . . but it would be even better if Michelle were here too.

KATE :   But then your Mum and Dad . . . . .

CHLOE :   My Mum's expecting another baby . . . . . d'you think that'll make them feel better about me?

KATE :   I think that's nice. I wish mine was.

CHLOE :   I wish I could see the baby though . . . . .

MANDY :   Well, maybe you will . . . . .

CHLOE :   How d'you mean?

MANDY :   We don't know much about this place yet, do we? We don't know what we might be able to do.

THE DECISION

> [GIRLS FREEZE AS ST PETER AND ANGEL MIME CONTINUATION OF DISCUSSION. THEY FREEZE IN TURN AS THE GIRLS UNFREEZE.]

KATE : We're not even in yet.

CHLOE : In?

KATE : Well, don't we have to be passed as good enough by Saint Peter?

MANDY : I presumed we were good enough and that's why we were brought here ..... except I shouldn't really be here.

KATE : D'you think they've sorted it out yet?

> [ST PETER AND ANGEL UNFREEZE. ANGEL MOVES AWAY FROM THE TABLE AND OVER TO THE GIRLS.]

ANGEL : Kate, Chloe, [SMILING.] If you two would like to have a drink at the ambrosia fountain over there; [POINTING IT OUT.] Peter would like another word with you, Mandy.

> [KATE AND CHLOE HURRY OVER TO THE FOUNTAIN AS ANGEL LEADS MANDY TO ST PETER. KATE AND CHLOE FREEZE.]

ST PETER : Do sit down, now ..... I'm in a bit of a predicament here, dear girl. And what I have to decide is – do I unite you and your twin up here and leave your parents to mourn their double loss or shall we leave Michelle to comfort them. She will, of course, no longer be able to dance, play tennis, walk even. [PAUSE.] How do you think she will cope?

THE DECISION

MANDY : She won't ..... she'll go mad: she lives for her dancing. Mum and Dad are so proud of her.

ST PETER : She will of course be made whole again when she eventually arrives here.

MANDY : Yes, but she doesn't know that, does she? I can't bear to think of her growing bitter ..... and ..... Oh ..... Saint Peter what will you decide?

[ST PETER AND MANDY FREEZE AS KATE AND CHLOE MIME THEIR EXCITEMENT AT THE DISCOVERY OF THE FOUNTAIN AND EXQUISITE DRINK. ST PETER AND MANDY UNFREEZE AND KATE AND CHLOE FREEZE IN TURN.

ST. PETER : Difficult is it not? There is of course a third way.

MANDY : Is there? What? Tell me please.

ST PETER : [TO ANGEL] It could be managed, couldn't it?

ANGEL : Well yes, if we were to act quickly.

ST PETER : Mandy will have to make the decision though.

ANGEL : Yes.

MANDY : But I can't if you don't tell me the third choice, can I?

ANGEL : We cannot tell you, I'm afraid. You must think of it for yourself.

THE DECISION

ST PETER :   We cannot return you to your earthly body but .....

MANDY :   Wait a minute ..... could I go back and swap places with Michelle? ..... I could bear it better than she could .... to be disabled I mean; now that I know about ..... 'up here'.

ST PETER :   Think about it very carefully. You will have to return to earth before Michelle regains consciousness if the exchange is to be made.

MANDY :   Can I say goodbye to Kate and Chloe before I go?

ST PETER :   Better they don't know. They would try and persuade you to stay here, wouldn't they?

MANDY :   I suppose so ..... but what about when Michelle arrives – won't they notice?

ANGEL :   They may realise perhaps, in time, but they'll know they can look forward to you rejoining them before too long.

MANDY :   [TO ST PETER.] But Saint Peter. you said seventy-one years.

ST PETER :   Time is different here.

ANGEL :   Seventy-one earth years are a mere 'hesitation' in a heavenly scheme.

MANDY :   Can I just see them for a minute?

THE DECISION

ST PETER : A moment only, or it will be too late. Go on then; your angel will collect you on the way down.

[ST PETER AND ANGEL FREEZE. CHLOE AND KATE UNFREEZE. AS MANDY HURRIES OVER TO JOIN THEM.]

MANDY : How was the ambrosia fountain?

CHLOE : Wonderful.

KATE : Scrummy: like all the most marvellous flavours you've ever tasted rolled into one delicious cold sparkling drink.

CHLOE : Come and have some.

MANDY : [HESITATING.] I don't think I'd better.

KATE : Why not?

MANDY : I'm going to see Michelle.

KATE : How d'you mean ..... see?

[THE ANGEL UNFREEZES AND BEGINS TO MOVE UNOBTRUSIVELY NEARER TO THE GIRLS.]

CHLOE : Isn't she coming up here?

MANDY : I don't know. Maybe not.

KATE : Can we come?

CHLOE : We could say proper goodbyes and tell people not to be sad and ..... that sort of thing.

THE DECISION

MANDY: I don't think you'll be allowed.

KATE: Why not?
CHLOE: If you are .....

MANDY: I don't really know. ..... Sorry.

CHLOE: It's probably because she's a twin.

KATE: Is it?

MANDY: Um ..... yes.

ANGEL: [APPEARING BEHIND THE GIRLS.] Ready?

[ST PETER UNFREEZES AND BEGINS TO MOVE UNOBTRUSIVELY NEARER TO CHLOE AND KATE.]

MANDY: Mmm.

KATE: She won't be long will she?

ANGEL: No ..... not long. [LEADS MANDY AWAY – MANDY BREAKS AWAY AND RUNS BACK TO HUG CHLOE AND KATE.]

MANDY: See you soon. [RUNS BACK TO ANGEL WHO TAKES HER HAND. THEY *EXIT.* AS ST PETER APPEARS BEHIND CHLOE AND KATE AND PUTS A HAND ON EACH OF THEIR SHOULDERS.]

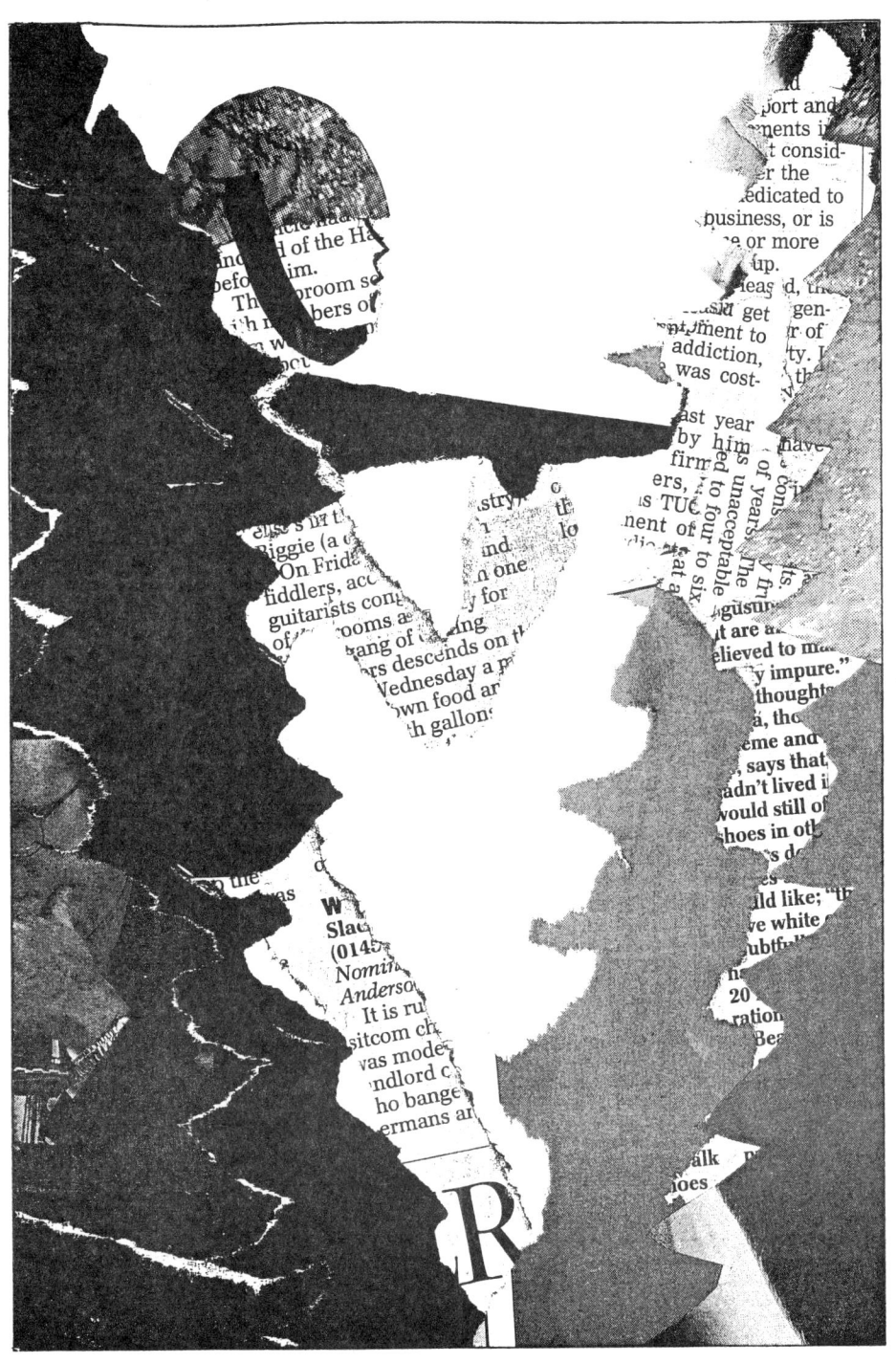

Goldilocks and the Three Burrs

7. Goldilocks And The Three Burrs

7 SHORT SCENES

NO OF PLAYERS : 5 • 6 • 7 + *
          [3 GIRLS + 2 BOYS
         4 GIRLS + 3 BOYS]
          * *OPTIONAL* NON-SPEAKING PLAYERS

CHARACTERS : GOLDILOCKS
        MOTHER
        MR BURR *
        MRS BURR *
        BENNY BURR *

        <u>NOTE</u> : MR BURR * MRS BURR * AND
        BENNY BURR * MAY DOUBLE AS TREES
        OR ADDITIONAL PLAYERS MAY BE USED.

        MALE DETECTIVE} MAY DOUBLE WITH
                MR BURR
        FEMALE DETECTIVE} MAY DOUBLE WITH
                MRS BURR

PROPS : <u>GOLDILOCKS'S HOUSE</u>
     CHAIR
     TELEPHONE

     <u>BURRS HIDEOUT</u>
     PORRIDGE POT AND SPOON
     PORRIDGE
     TABLE AND 3 CHAIRS
     PLACE SETTINGS FOR 3
     JACKET

     DAISIES
     MOBILE PHONE

GOLDILOCKS AND THE THREE BURRS

SOUND : GUN SHOTS

SCENE ONE : GOLDILOCKS'S HOUSE. [TO ONE SIDE OF PERFORMING AREA.]

MOTHER • GOLDILOCKS

MOTHER : Breakfast will be at least half an hour, I'm afraid.

GOLDILOCKS : I'm ever so hungry.

MOTHER : It's a lovely morning. Why don't you go for a walk?

GOLDILOCKS : That'll make me even hungrier.

MOTHER : Well, take an apple or something.

GOLDILOCKS : [SULKILY.] I suppose so.

MOTHER : Keep to the fields, mind. Don't go into the forest.

GOLDILOCKS : Right you are, Mummy. See you later.

MOTHER : [KISSING GOLDILOCKS.] 'Bye, dear.

[GOLDILOCKS *EXITS.*]

SCENE TWO : MEANWHILE – AT THE COTTAGE HIDEOUT. [THE OPPOSITE SIDE OF PERFORMING AREA.]

MR BURR • MRS BURR • BENNY • GOLDILOCKS

MR BURR : There's just one more load to fetch. I'd like to get it done today.

GOLDILOCKS AND THE THREE BURRS

BENNY: Can we have breakfast first?

MR BURR: No. I want to get them shifted before anybody's around.

MRS BURR: I'll just put some porridge on before we go then; I've already made some sandwiches for the journey.

MR BURR: Right then! Five minutes and we're off. Benny – you'd better come too – you can help fill the pit in when we've retrieved the rifles.

BENNY: Oh Da-ad!

MR BURR: Don't argue.

[MR BURR *EXITS.*]

MRS BURR: Go and help move the camouflage off the van.

BENNY: Okay, then. [SHOUTING.] Coming Dad. [BENNY *EXITS.*]

[MRS BURR MAKES PORRIDGE, LAYS THE TABLE, ETC. MR. BURR AND BENNY *RE-ENTER* AS TREES – THEN MRS. BURR BECOMES ONE.]

NOTE: ALTERNATIVELY MRS BURR *EXITS* AND NON-SPEAKING PLAYERS *ENTER* AS TREES.

[GOLDILOCKS *ENTERS* PICKING DAISIES AND STRAYS INTO THE FOREST AND STARTS TO WEAVE AMONG THE TREES WHICH MELT AWAY WHEN SHE FINDS THE HIDEOUT.]

GOLDILOCKS: Coo-ee! Anyone at home? I think I'm lost. [WALKING IN.] Can I come in?

93

GOLDILOCKS AND THE THREE BURRS

[ROUTINE OF TRYING PORRIDGE, BREAKING CHAIRS, ETC – SHE THEN LOOKS OUT OF THE WINDOW TO SEE THE BURRS RETURNING.]

GOLDILOCKS : [GASPS REGISTERING SHOCK AT WHAT SHE SEES.] Oh! <u>Guns</u>! [SHE HIDES.]

SCENE THREE : MEANWHILE - BACK AT THE HOUSE.

MOTHER

[GOLDILOCKS'S MOTHER IS ON THE PHONE.]

MOTHER : Good heavens! Terrorists? ..... What? – round here? Are you sure? ..... No, I haven't got my morning paper yet. ..... Well of course I'm worried – Goldilocks went out for a walk near the forest and she's not back yet.

[SHE PUTS THE PHONE DOWN, PACES UP AND DOWN AND THEN SITS WITH HER HEAD IN HER HANDS]

SCENE 4 : MEANWHILE - BACK AT THE HIDEOUT.

GOLDILOCKS • MR BURR • MRS BURR • BENNY

[BURR FAMILY *ENTER*]

MR BURR : What the heck?

MRS BURR : Someone's been in.

MR BURR : Did you lock the door Benny?

BENNY : I thought I did after Mum got in the van.

GOLDILOCKS AND THE THREE BURRS

MR. BURR :   Blithering idiot! [LOOKS AS IF HE MIGHT HIT BENNY.]

MRS BURR :   Oh leave him alone Bert. We'd better see if anything's missing.

MR BURR :   What about those hand grenades?

MRS BURR :   Where did you put them?

MR BURR :   Cupboard in the hall.

MRS BURR :   [LOOKING.] It's alright they're still there.

MR BURR :   I think we'd better get out of here as quickly as possible.

MRS BURR :   What about breakfast?

MR BURR :   Sod breakfast.

MRS BURR :   Bert, really!

BENNY :   I'm hungry.

MR BURR :   Shut up! Go and check the windows are shut and fetch anything you need for the journey. [TO MRS BURR.] help me get the rest of the stuff into the van.

SCENE FIVE :   MEANWHILE - BACK AT GOLDILOCKS'S HOUSE

MOTHER

[MOTHER IS ON THE PHONE TO THE POLICE.]

GOLDILOCKS AND THE THREE BURRS

MOTHER : ..... Yes - she's been missing for well over an hour. ..... I know, but she hasn't had breakfast [PAUSE.] and we live just by the forest where those terrorists might be hiding. ..... Oh, would you? ..... Yes, I'll stay here. Please hurry . . . .Thank you.

SCENE SIX : MEANWHILE - BACK AT THE HIDEOUT

GOLDILOCKS • BENNY • MR BURR • MRS BURR

[GOLDILOCKS IS HIDING UPSTAIRS. SHE SNEEZES. BENNY IS FETCHING A JACKET FROM THE ROOM HEARS GOLDILOCKS SNEEZE AND FINDS HER.]

BENNY : What the ..... ? 'Ere who are you?

GOLDILOCKS : [STUTTERING.] Gggoldilllocks.

BENNY : Pull the other one.

GOLDILOCKS: Please don't give me away.

BENNY : Dad'll do you in, if he finds you here.

GOLDILOCKS : Please ..... please ..... let me go.

MR BURR : [SHOUTING FROM OFF-STAGE.] Hurry up, Benny for Pete's sake, or do I have to come up and drag you down?

BENNY : Just coming, Dad.

GOLDILOCKS : Your dad wouldn't really kill me would he?

GOLDILOCKS AND THE THREE BURRS

BENNY: He might, although Mum might try and stop him.

GOLDILOCKS: Is she here too?

BENNY: Yeah .....

MR BURR: [SHOUTING FROM OFF-STAGE.] Benny get your bleeding self bleedin' down here.

GOLDILOCKS: Oh, please help me.

BENNY: We could climb out the window.

GOLDILOCKS: I don't know my way out of the forest.

BENNY: I'll show you. ..... Come on – before Dad comes.

[MR BURR AND MRS. BURR *ENTER* AS TREES.]

NOTE: ALTERNATIVELY NON-SPEAKING PLAYERS *ENTER* AS TREES.

[GOLDILOCKS AND BENNY WEAVE BETWEEN TREES MAKING THEIR WAY THROUGH THE FOREST. FINALLY THEY SEE GOLDILOCKS'S HOUSE. THE TREES THEN DISAPPEAR.]

GOLDILOCKS: There's my house. [SHE GASPS.] There's a police car outside.

BENNY: [NERVOUSLY.] I'd better scarper.

GOLDILOCKS: Won't you come in with me?

BENNY: Can't risk getting nicked ..... got to go ..... ta-raa. [HE *EXITS* HASTILY.]

GOLDILOCKS AND THE THREE BURRS

SCENE SEVEN: MEANWHILE - BACK AT THE HOUSE.

GOLDILOCKS • MOTHER • MALE DETECTIVE • FEMALE DETECTIVE

[GOLDILOCK'S MUM LOOKS OUT OF THE DOOR AND SEES GOLDILOCKS RETURNING. TWO DETECTIVES HOVER IN BACKGROUND.]

GOLDILOCKS : [RUSHING INTO MOTHER'S ARMS.] Oh Mummy! Mummy! I was so scared.

MOTHER : Darling, whatever's happened. Are you hurt?

GOLDILOCKS : I'm ..... I'm ..... Benny saved me.

MOTHER : Who's Benny?

GOLDILOCKS : He's gone and I never said thank you.

MOTHER : But who is he?

[THE TWO DETECTIVES STEP FORWARD.]

MALE DI : Is this your daughter madam?

MOTHER : [CLASPING GOLDILOCKS.] Yes, yes – this is Goldilocks.

MALE DI : We would like to ask her a few questions.

FEMALE DI : Just a few.

MALE DI : We have a team out now searching the forest and your daughter may be able to give us some valuable information.

GOLDILOCKS AND THE THREE BURRS

MOTHER : Don't you think she's been through enough?

MALE DI : We just want to catch these terrorists as soon as possible.

MOTHER : All right. Do you feel up to answering a few questions darling?

GOLDILOCKS : I'm okay, Mummy.

FEMALE DI : Do you know how many there were?

GOLDILOCKS : Two I think, and Benny of course.

MOTHER :
FEMALE DI : } Who's Benny?
MALE DI :

GOLDILOCKS : Their little boy – he helped me to escape.

FEMALE DI : Where is he now?

GOLDILOCKS : He ran back to find his parents.

MALE DI : Silly blighter, he'll get himself shot.

MOTHER : <u>Shot</u>?

GOLDILOCKS : You mustn't let them shoot him – you mustn't.

MOTHER : Now then, now then darling, you mustn't upset yourself.

GOLDILOCKS : But Mummy – if they shoot Benny.

MOTHER : [TO DETECTIVES.] Can't you do anything?

GOLDILOCKS AND THE THREE BURRS

[MOTHER COMFORTS GOLDILOCKS.]

MALE DI :   We'll do our best madam. [SPEAKS QUIETLY AND VERY BRIEFLY ON MOBILE PHONE. FINISHES WITH.] ..... If you see a young male trying to reach the terrorists, hold your fire.

MOTHER :   [SUDDENLY THINKS.] Can I get you all a cup of tea?

MALE DI :   Thank you, madam.

FEMALE DI :   That would be very welcome, a nice cup of tea. Thank you, madam.

MOTHER :   [TO GOLDILOCKS.] Would you like anything dear?

GOLDILOCKS :   I'm quite full actually, Mummy.

[FROM OFF-STAGE SOUNDS OF GUN SHOTS. ALL TURN TO LOOK AS BENNY *ENTERS*. HE STAGGERS IN AND COLLAPSES. ALL MOVE NEARER HIM.]

GOLDILOCKS :   [RUSHING TO CROUCH BY BENNY.] ..... Benny .....

The Queen from Alice and the Mushrooms

8. Alice And The Mushrooms

4 SHORT SCENES

NO OF PLAYERS : 5 • 6 • 7 + *
        [1 - 3 BOYS + 2 - 4 GIRLS
        ALL GIRLS]
        * *OPTIONAL* NON-SPEAKING PLAYERS

CHARACTERS : ALICE
                DAISY
                RABBIT
                CATERPILLAR
                HATTER
                QUEEN
                DUCHESS

NOTE : QUEEN] MAY DOUBLE WITH DAISY
        DUCHESS] MAY DOUBLE WITH DAISY

PROPS : WATERING CAN
        A TRUG OR BASKET FILLED WITH MUSHROOMS

SCENE ONE : A WOOD LEADING TO A CLEARING.

                DAISY • ALICE

                NOTE: THE REMAINING PLAYERS ARE TREES AND MAKE "WIND WHISTLING" SOUNDS

                [*ENTER* DAISY AND ALICE WALKING TOGETHER.]

DAISY :   I hope we find somewhere soon.

ALICE :   I'm getting hungry.

DAISY :   Do keep up Alice, or you'll get lost.

ALICE AND THE MUSHROOMS

ALICE: My feet hurt.

DAISY: I promise we'll stop as soon as we find a gap in these trees.

[SOUNDS OFF-STAGE.]

ALICE: Daisy, I'm frightened.

DAISY: There's nothing to worry about, as long as you keep up.

ALICE: I thought I heard something.

DAISY: Probably the wind in the trees.

ALICE: I'm sure something's following us.

DAISY: It's just your vivid imagination dear. Do come on. [FINDS A PLACE.] Now look, here's a lovely spot. You sit down and I'll pick some daisies, then you can make a daisy chain, whilst I fetch some water from that stream we passed.

[EXIT DAISY. TREES MELT AWAY.]

SCENE TWO : THE CLEARING IN THE WOOD

ALICE • RABBIT • HATTER • CATERPILLAR • QUEEN • DUCHESS

[ALICE FALLS ASLEEP. ENTER RABBIT.]

RABBIT: Dear me ..... dear me. They must be somewhere. The Queen will have my guts for garters if I don't find them.

ALICE AND THE MUSHROOMS

[SEES ALICE.] Good heavens! Where did that come from? It's a small person I think! Probably lying on my mushrooms. [COUGHING.] Hmm! Hmm! Excuse me, small person.

ALICE : [WAKING WITH A START.] Oh! Where am I?

RABBIT : I think you may be lying on them.

ALICE : Lying on them? [SHE SITS UP.]

RABBIT : They'll be all squashed.

ALICE : What will?

RABBIT : She'll be so cross.

ALICE : Who will?

RABBIT : The Queen of course.

ALICE : The Queen?

RABBIT : We're having them creamed, on toast, for tea, you see.

ALICE : Are we?

RABBIT : No, not you.

ALICE : Who?

RABBIT : The Queen is.

ALICE : The Queen is what?

RABBIT : Very cross when she doesn't get them.

ALICE AND THE MUSHROOMS

ALICE: Get who?

RABBIT: No, not who, silly small person.

ALICE: I'm feeling very confused.

RABBIT: Quite natural.

ALICE: Is it?

RABBIT: Oh yes, compulsory really.

ALICE: Really?

RABBIT: Yes of course, the Hatter is the most confused. And the Caterpillar is not usually far behind.

ALICE: Far behind what?

RABBIT: Far behind the mushrooms of course. That is why I must find them before he gets here. He's a very fast eater, you know.

[*EXIT* RABBIT. ALICE SINKS DOWN AND IMMEDIATELY FALLS ASLEEP AGAIN. *ENTER* HATTER AND CATERPILLAR.]

HATTER: What o'clock is it?

CATERPILLAR: Half past.

HATTER: Half past what?

CATERPILLAR: Half past tea-time.

HATTER: You are always thinking about your stomach.

ALICE AND THE MUSHROOMS

CATERPILLAR: My stomach likes me to think of it at least six times a day.

HATTER: I shouldn't think there's much room left in your stomach after that huge bowl of forlorn cakes you had for breakfast.

CATERPILLAR: Much room! Much room! Always room for mushrooms. Mushrooms on toast. Yum! Yum!

HATTER: I hope you haven't been picking the Queen's mushrooms again?

CATERPILLAR: Well, no, there were still plenty there when I .....

HATTER: When you?

CATERPILLAR: When I borrowed .....

HATTER: Borrowed? How many did you "borrow"?

CATERPILLAR: One or two ..... [HATTER LOOKS AT CATERPILLAR HARD.] ..... or three.

HATTER: Are there any left?

CATERPILLAR: A few just ..... [SEES ALICE.] just .... um ..... Oh! ..... there seems to be a small person lying um .....

HATTER: Lying um?

CATERPILLAR: Lying on the last of the mushrooms.

HATTER: The Queen is going to be .....

105

ALICE AND THE MUSHROOMS

HATTER : CATERPILLAR : }	Furious!
ALICE :	[WAKING SUDDENLY.] Who? ..... Who are you? [SHE SITS UP.]
HATTER :	More to the point who are you?
ALICE :	I'm Alice.
CATERPILLAR :	Where have you come from?
ALICE :	I'm not sure.
HATTER :	The seashore?
ALICE :	No, [POINTING.] from over there.
HATTER :	Oh! You mean Thursday.
ALICE :	I'm not sure when I started. We were going to have a picnic.
CATERPILLAR :	Is that something to eat?
ALICE :	Yes.
CATERPILLAR :	In a basket?
ALICE :	Yes
CATERPILLAR :	Mushrooms?
ALICE :	Sorry?
CATERPILLAR :	Do you have mushrooms in your basket?
ALICE :	No, sandwiches.

ALICE AND THE MUSHROOMS

CATERPILLAR : <u>No</u> Sandwiches? Well never mind, but do you have mushrooms?

ALICE : No, I have sandwiches.

CATERPILLAR : Why didn't you say so.

ALICE : I'm feeling confused again.

HATTER : Quite natural. Compulsory really.

ALICE : That's what he said.

CATERPILLAR : No, I didn't.

ALICE : No, not you.

CATERPILLAR : Who?

ALICE : Um ..... long ears ..... um ..... whiskers ..... um .....

QUEEN : [<u>VOICE</u> OFF-STAGE.] Where is my white rabbit?

[*ENTER* QUEEN.]

QUEEN : Where is my rabbit?

[*ENTER* RABBIT.]

RABBIT : [RUSHING ON BREATHLESS.] H ..... here Your M ..... majesty.

QUEEN : Have you found them yet?

RABBIT : Not ..... quite, ma'am.

ALICE AND THE MUSHROOMS

QUEEN : Not quite! Not quite! When did you expect to do so? The toast will be ready soon, you know.

RABBIT : Sh ..... sh she's sitting on them.

QUEEN : Is she? What for? Is she keeping them warm? Where did she come from anyway?

HATTER : She doesn't seem to know, Your M ..... Majesty.

CATERPILLAR : Very confused, ma'am.

QUEEN : Ah well, that's a start. Up you get, quickly!

RABBIT : [TO ALICE.] A small curtsey would be appropriate.

QUEEN : That's it. Now that you're up my rabbit can get down [FALSE LAUGH Ha! Ha!] to picking mushrooms.

RABBIT : Certainly ma'am. At once ma'am. [HE LOOKS AND RECOILS IN HORROR.] Oh, my goodness. They're not there.

QUEEN : What! Have you eaten them, little girl?

ALICE : No your majesty. I brought sandwiches.

QUEEN : But it's Saturday.

RABBIT : I'm terribly sorry ma'am. P .... Perhaps you would care for a sandwich? ..... ma'am?

ALICE AND THE MUSHROOMS

QUEEN : I <u>ALWAYS</u> have mushrooms on toast on Saturdays.

CATERPILLAR : I'm sure they are very good sandwiches, Your Majesty. [TO ALICE.]. What sort of sandwiches are they, small person?

ALICE : Well there's potted meat, marmalade, chocolate .....

HATTER : Sounds excellent, your majesty?

QUEEN : No, no, no. I will not be fobbed off with nursery food. When I say I want <u>MUSHROOMS</u> on toast, I mean mushrooms on toast. And if I don't get my mushrooms on toast there will be ..... [LOOKING HARD AT RABBIT.]

RABBIT : T..... T ..... trouble your majesty.

QUEEN : I shall be ..... [LOOKING HARD AT HATTER.]

HATTER : Extremely angry, ma'am.

CATERPILLAR : Very hungry ma'am.

QUEEN : Precisely. So look lively. Stir your stumps. More mushrooms must be found by four o'clock ..... precisely.

[*EXIT* QUEEN.]

RABBIT :
HATTER : } Precisely.
CATERPILLAR :

[ALL TURN TO ALICE.]

ALICE AND THE MUSHROOMS

RABBIT : ⎫
HATTER : ⎬ It's your fault, you know.
CATERPILLAR : ⎭

ALICE : How is it my fault?

HATTER : You must have squashed them.

RABBIT : Whatever shall we do?

ALICE : [LOOKING ON THE GROUND.] I don't see any sign of them.

CATERPILLAR : I'm sure there were some left when ..

HATTER : Caterpillar, just how many did you take?

RABBIT : Did you eat them all?

ALICE : Arguing won't find more mushrooms. Is there anywhere else they grow?

HATTER : Don't think so.

CATERPILLAR : I've never found anywhere else.

HATTER : And I'm sure you've looked!

CATERPILLAR : I always keep an eye open for them in the course of my perambulations through the wood. [OTHERS STARE HARD AT CATERPILLAR.]

RABBIT : I did hear the Duchess was trying to cultivate them in her herb garden.

ALICE : Is that near here?

ALICE AND THE MUSHROOMS

RABBIT : Nobody is quite sure. Her garden is invisible to most people.

ALICE : Well, how shall we find it?

HATTER : We must listen very carefully. If she's in a good mood one can sometimes hear her singing.

CATERPILLAR : Can one? Can two?

HATTER : Well we might if you keep quiet and, [LOOKING AT RABBIT WHO IS JIGGLING ABOUT NERVOUSLY.] very, very still.

[THEY ALL FREEZE. DUCHESS IS HEARD SINGING IS FROM FAR OFF.]

ALICE : Is that her?

RABBIT : Yes, yes, follow me.

[THEY ALL *EXIT* AS DUCHESS *ENTERS* WITH A WATERING CAN, A TRUG, ETC.]

SCENE THREE : THE INVISIBLE GARDEN

DUCHESS • RABBIT • HATTER • CATERPILLAR • ALICE

NOTE : DUCHESS SONG IS *OPTIONAL*. THE RHYME MAY BE SPOKEN.

DUCHESS : Mary, Mary, quite contrary,
How does your garden grow?
With silver bells and cockle shells,
And pretty maids all in a row.

ALICE AND THE MUSHROOMS

[*ENTER* RABBIT, HATTER, CATERPILLAR AND ALICE.]

RABBIT:
HATTER:
CATERPILLAR:
ALICE: } [ARRIVING.] Here she is.

DUCHESS: Quiet! Quiet! I am propagating.

HATTER: Beg pardon ma'am. Proper what?

DUCHESS: Propagating, you buffoon. Mulching mushrooms.

CATERPILLAR: Mushrooms?

DUCHESS: Are you deaf?

CATERPILLAR: Beg pardon, ma'am.

DUCHESS: Granted, granted.

RABBIT: By any chance . . . . .

CATERPILLAR: We wondered if . . . . .

HATTER: Are you selling them ma'am?

DUCHESS: Shelling them? Of course not. One doesn't shell mushrooms you know.

ALICE: We'd love some mushrooms.

DUCHESS: They are attractive aren't they? They should be ready by morning.

RABBIT: Not till then, ma'am?

ALICE AND THE MUSHROOMS

DUCHESS: Not till then. Now off you go ..... quietly now. They need perfect peace while they are germinating.

CATERPILLAR: [TO HATTER.] What does that mean?

HATTER: Don't ask me.

CATERPILLAR: I am asking you.

ALICE: I'm afraid I don't know either.

DUCHESS: Quiet!

[THEY QUIVER. RABBIT, HATTER AND CATERPILLAR *EXIT*.]

ALICE: I'm sorry ma'am ..... but it's the Queen's tea, you see.

DUCHESS: Ah! Is it Saturday?

ALICE: I think so.

DUCHESS: That explains it. I suppose the caterpillar's eaten them again.

ALICE: I think I may have squashed some ..... by accident of course.

DUCHESS: Tut! Tut! She won't do without her mushrooms. I suppose I could let you have some I picked earlier.

ALICE: Could you really? Oh that would be kind.

DUCHESS: Don't mention it dear. Here you are.
[HANDING ALICE A TRUG OF MUSHROOMS.]
Now I must go. Heigh-ho!

ALICE AND THE MUSHROOMS

[DUCHESS *EXITS.*]

ALICE :   [LOOKING AROUND.] Oh! They've all disappeared. I don't know my way back. [CALLING.] Rabbit? Hatter? Caterpillar? Hello, is anyone there? Oh dear, what shall I do?

[RABBIT, CATERPILLAR AND HATTER RUN ACROSS THE PERFORMANCE AREA IN TURN AND ALICE TRIES TO STOP THEM.]

ALICE :   Rabbit, wait, please ..... Oh Hatter ..... I have some mushrooms. ..... Caterpillar please, don't go ..... Wait ..... Wait!

[SHE TRIPS AND THE MUSHROOMS SPILL OUT OF THE TRUG. SHE FAINTS INTO SLEEP.]

SCENE FOUR :   THE CLEARING IN THE WOOD.

DAISY • ALICE • AND ALL THE PLAYERS

[ALICE SLEEPS. DAISY *ENTERS.*]

DAISY :   [SHAKING ALICE.] Alice ..... Alice ..... Alice. Wake up!

ALICE :   What? ..... The mushrooms, the mushrooms.

DAISY :   Alice, what are you talking about?

ALICE :   The Hatter, the Caterpillar, the Rabbit, the Queen. Where are they?

DAISY :   You've been dreaming again, Alice.

ALICE AND THE MUSHROOMS

ALICE : But it seemed so real.

[ON "SO REAL" – ALL THE OTHER PLAYERS *ENTER* AND PASS BEHIND DAISY AND ALICE MIMING "SH!" TO THE AUDIENCE.]

The Art Gallery 2

9. The Art Gallery

NO OF PLAYERS : 6
                    [1 - 4 BOYS + 2 - 5 GIRLS

CHARACTERS : DRAGON
                  SAINT GEORGE
                  MAIDEN
                  CURATOR
                  CHILD ONE
                  CHILD TWO

COSTUMES/PROPS : <u>ST GEORGE</u>
                      ARMOUR **
                      A LANCE TO CARRY

                      <u>MAIDEN</u>
                      GOWN **
                      A WHITE LILY TO CARRY

                      <u>DRAGON</u>
                      GREEN COSTUME WITH LONG TAIL ***
                      *** NO BACK FEET
                      HEAD-DRESS OR MASK

** SPLIT DOWN THE BACK WITH VELCRO FASTENING FOR LIGHTNING QUICK CHANGE AND TO FIT OVER CHILD ONE AND CHILD TWO'S CLOTHING. ST. GEORGE WEARS SHIRT, ETC. UNDER ARMOUR (OR AMUSING UNDERWEAR) AND MAIDEN LONG PETTICOATS.

                      OVERSIZED PICTURE FRAME *
                      CUPBOARD *
                            * *OPTIONAL*
                      FEATHER DUSTER/DUSTER
                      ARTISTS SKETCH PAD
                      FOLDING CHAIR/STOOL
                      BOX OF PENCILS/PENCIL-CASE
                      PAIR OF GLASSES

THE ART GALLERY

> WATCH
> LARGE BUNCH OF KEYS

SCENE : A GALLERY OF PAINTINGS IN A MUSEUM.

[DRAGON, ST GEORGE AND THE MAIDEN - LOOKING FRIGHTENED, ARE POSED AS IN A TRADITIONAL PICTURE INSIDE THE PICTURE FRAME.]

DRAGON : Have they gone?

ST GEORGE : Who?

DRAGON : That noisy pack of children.

ST GEORGE : Another school party. Yes, they're gone.

DRAGON : Thank goodness. My eczema's playing me up again. I just must have a scratch.

ST GEORGE : I thought it was better after that linseed oil treatment they gave you in the restoration shop.

DRAGON : No they missed all the bits that don't show, you know.

ST GEORGE : I must say, I think I could have done with a bit more oil on the joints of this armour of mine.

DRAGON : And there's some paint flaking off my tail which you, by the way, are treading on.

ST GEORGE : Sorry, sorry – I just had to move. I keep getting cramp.

THE ART GALLERY

MAIDEN: [SNEEZING.] Stop grumbling you two. You're giving me a headache. I'm sure I've a cold coming on. They made my gown sopping wet when they touched up the fabric. The paint was far too thin.

DRAGON: They dilute it with turpentine. It really made my eyes water.

MAIDEN: And those sable brushes tickle frightfully.

ST GEORGE: I thought I heard you giggling.

MAIDEN: It was no laughing matter but I couldn't help it.

DRAGON: Talking about tickling, could you just scratch my back with your lance, George?

ST GEORGE: Be my guest. [HE SCRATCHES DRAGON'S BACK.]

DRAGON: Bit lower ..... slightly to the left ..... ah ..... that's mmm ..... much better.

[*ENTER* CURATOR. ST GEORGE TRIES TO REPOSITION HIS LANCE BUT IT FALLS OUT OF THE PICTURE.]

CURATOR: [LOOKS AROUND – SPOTS LANCE ON FLOOR.] What on earth's that doing in here. If those dratted children have been mucking about in the armour room again .....

[HE PICKS LANCE UP – STANDS WITH BACK TO PICTURE. MAIDEN TICKLES HIM UNDER THE ARM OR BACK OF NECK WITH HER LILY. HE JERKS. ST GEORGE RETRIEVES LANCE.]

THE ART GALLERY

CURATOR : What the? ..... [LOOKS AROUND AND SCRATCHES HIS HEAD - *EXITS.*]

ST GEORGE : That was a close one.

DRAGON : You're telling me.

MAIDEN : You really should be more careful.

ST GEORGE : He/She never suspects us. He/She doesn't know what day of the week it is.

DRAGON : Neither do I if it comes to that. Don't much care either. [BIG SIGH.]

MAIDEN: Are you feeling a bit depressed again.

DRAGON : Mmmmm. [SNIFF.]

MAIDEN : Oh – don't .....

DRAGON : It's all very well, but you don't know what it's like being unpopular for hundreds of years.

MAIDEN : Well, I like you.

DRAGON : Do you?

MAIDEN : Of course I do.

DRAGON : What about that look of terror on your face?

MAIDEN : That's just acting.

DRAGON : Is it?

MAIDEN : You know it is. I quite fancy you really.

THE ART GALLERY

ST GEORGE : Here, steady on! You're supposed to fancy me.

MAIDEN : Just acting, sunshine.

ST GEORGE : Are you?

MAIDEN : Wouldn't you like to know?

ST GEORGE : Yes I would.

[*ENTER* CURATOR WITH DUSTER.]

MAIDEN : Sh! Curator's back.

[CURATOR WONDERS AROUND, DUSTS A BIT, ETC. GETS **GALLERY CLOSED SIGN** OUT AS CHILD ONE *ENTERS.* – CARRYING A SKETCH PAD.]

CURATOR : Sorry miss. Can't come in here now; Gallery's closed for half an hour.

CHILD ONE: But Miss Smith sent me.

CURATOR : Now why was that?

CHILD ONE: She told me off for laughing.

CURATOR : And what were you laughing at then?

CHILD ONE: Bare ..... [GIGGLE.] eating outside.

CURATOR : Bears? Outside here?

CHILD ONE: [GIGGLING.] No, no - not bears. Naked people having lunch.

CURATOR : Where?

THE ART GALLERY

CHILD ONE: Outside.

CURATOR: In this weather?!

CHILD ONE: No, outside in the picture. Having a picnic with no clothes on!

CURATOR: [DAWNING.] Was this in the gallery upstairs?

CHILD: Yes.

CURATOR: Ah. That explains it. [PRONOUNCING BADLY.] "Déjeuner sur l'herbe" ..... or, to translate, lunch on the grass. ..... Did you like the painting?

CHILD ONE: I thought it was funny, and I said to Sally – wouldn't it be a giggle if the teachers didn't wear anything on the school picnic ..... and Sally said she thought one of the ladies in the picture looked like Miss Smith and then everyone started giggling and I got sent out, and she says I have to sit in here and draw something.

CURATOR: Well, I suppose it'd be alright if you promise not to run about and touch things.

CHILD ONE: I promise.

CURATOR: What would you like to draw?

CHILD ONE: [LOOKING AROUND.] I like that dragon.

CURATOR: Yes, he's quite popular with people.

THE ART GALLERY

MAIDEN : [MAIDEN NUDGES DRAGON.] See!

[ST GEORGE GRIMACES. CURATOR FETCHES CHAIR FOR CHILD ONE.]

CURATOR : Well I'll be back soon. Remember, no touching things.

CHILD : No I won't.

[*EXIT* CURATOR.]

[CHILD ONE STARTS DRAWING – WHILST SHE/HE'S GETTING ANOTHER PENCIL OUT OF BOX ST GEORGE SIGHS AND MOVES HIS LANCE TO HIS OTHER HAND.]

[CHILD TWO *ENTERS.*]

CHILD TWO : What are you drawing?

CHILD ONE : This dragon and Saint George.

CHILD TWO : Oh! [STUDIES DRAWING.] . . . . .
You've got his lance in the wrong hand.

CHILD ONE : No I haven't.

CHILD TWO : Yes you have.

CHILD ONE : [LOOKING AT PICTURE.] Well, I . . . . . that's funny. I'm sure I . . . . . Bother, I'll have to start again.

CHILD TWO : Doesn't really matter I suppose.

CHILD ONE : And I'm having great difficulty with this dragon . . . . . he's a really odd shape.

DRAGON : [INDIGNANTLY.] No I'm not.

THE ART GALLERY

CHILD ONE :   [TO CHILD TWO.] What did you say?

CHILD TWO :   Didn't say anything. ..... When?

CHILD ONE :   After I said about the dragon being a funny shape.

DRAGON :   You're a funny shape.

CHILD TWO :   [TO CHILD ONE.] Sorry?

CHILD ONE :   What are you on about?

CHILD TWO :   Did you say I was a funny shape?

DRAGON :   No. I said she was.

[CHILD ONE AND CHILD TWO LOOK AT DRAGON THEN AT EACH OTHER.]

CHILD ONE : ⎫   ..... Did you? ..... Uh?
CHILD TWO : ⎭   .... He .....

[THEY START BACKING AWAY.]

MAIDEN :   Don't go away. He won't hurt you.

CHILD ONE :   Are you really talking?

CHILD TWO :   To us?

MAIDEN :   Yes. You don't mind do you? Only we get a bit bored with each other's company ..... together all day every day. You understand?

CHILD ONE :   Yes. ..... But how are you talking? You're not real.

THE ART GALLERY

ST GEORGE: Who's not real?

CHILD TWO: You. You're a painting.

MAIDEN: We were very real once. A long time ago, in Italy. I was the artist's girlfriend.

ST GEORGE: I was his best mate.

CHILD ONE: Where is he now?

ST GEORGE: Who?

CHILD ONE: The artist.

ST GEORGE: Oh he died years and years ago, but he immortalised us you see.

CHILD TWO: Immortalised?

MAIDEN: Made us live forever.

DRAGON: And ever and ever.

CHILD ONE: Even you?

DRAGON: Why not?

CHILD ONE: Well you're not so realistic, and you were hardly the artist's pet dinosaur, were you?

DRAGON: I was the product of a fertile imagination, a hybrid of iguanodon, pterodactyl and brontosaurus.

MAIDEN: In fact, unique: he's lovely isn't he?

CHILD TWO: Well, he's a lovely colour certainly.

THE ART GALLERY

MAIDEN : Trouble is he suffers from depression.

DRAGON : We don't get out much.

MAIDEN : I wonder ..... I've just had a thought. You two wouldn't consider doing us a <u>little</u> favour would you?

CHILD ONE : What sort of favour?

MAIDEN : If you could just come and be me for a few minutes, there's a rather dishy young man called Narcissus, in the next gallery.

ST GEORGE : I don't know why you want to bother with him. The only thing he admires is himself ..... stares at his own reflection all day long.

CHILD TWO : Oh yes, we did learn about him - in Myths and Legends.

MAIDEN : I'd still like to try .....

ST GEORGE : I'll come with you. I'd like to stretch my legs.

MAIDEN : Well, go and stretch them somewhere else.

DRAGON : What about me?

MAIDEN : You can stay and talk to the children.

[GEORGE AND MAIDEN CLIMB OUT OF THE PICTURE. THE CHILDREN HELP THEM OUT OF THEIR CLOTHING AND THEY IN TURN HELP THE CHILDREN INTO THE RELEVANT GARB AS CHILD ONE BECOMES MAIDEN AND

THE ART GALLERY

                    CHILD TWO ST GEORGE. CHILD ONE THEN CLIMBS INTO PAINTING. CHILD TWO IS LEFT OUTSIDE FRAME ADJUSTING ARMOUR AS ST GEORGE AND MAIDEN SIDLE OFF AND *EXIT*.]

CHILD ONE: [TO CHILD TWO.] Hurry up into the picture – the Curator will be back soon. He/She might notice.

DRAGON: He/She never notices much. Oh, I hear him/her coming. Quickly – keep still.

                    [CHILD ONE FREEZES IN THE PICTURE – CHILD TWO FREEZES OUTSIDE FRAME *ENTER* CURATOR.]

CURATOR: [NOTICING SUIT OF ARMOUR.] Those dratted children! And where's that little girl/boy who was drawing? [TAKING HOLD OF ARMOUR.] Better get this locked away till we find where it's come from.

                    [CURATOR WALKS ARMOUR WITH CHILD TWO INSIDE TO CUPBOARD, SELECTS A KEY FROM BUNCH AND LOCKS IT IN.. *EXITS*.]

CHILD ONE: [WHISPERING TO DRAGON.] What shall we do?

DRAGON: Keep still till the others get back. They'll know what to do.

CHILD ONE: I hope they won't be long.

DRAGON: Don't worry.

CHILD ONE: I am worrying. What if Miss Smith comes back?

THE ART GALLERY

DRAGON :   The lady who disapproves of laughing?

CHILD ONE :   That's the one.

               [*ENTER* MAIDEN.]

MAIDEN :   [BREEZILY ON ENTERING.] Everything all right?

DRAGON :   Um, not ..... um ..... quite.

CHILD ONE :   He's taken my friend.

MAIDEN :   Who has?

CHILD ONE :   The Curator ..... and locked him/her up.

DRAGON :   In Saint George's armour.

MAIDEN :   Oh! ..... how awkward.

DRAGON :   Where's George?

MAIDEN :   Trying to chat up the cloakroom attendant.

DRAGON :   That sounds about right.

MAIDEN :   What are we going to do?

DRAGON :   Well I can't do anything can I?

MAIDEN :   No, I suppose not.

CHILD ONE :   Why not?

DRAGON :   The artist didn't ..... [SNIFF.] ..... didn't .....

THE ART GALLERY

MAIDEN : Didn't give him any hind feet, poor thing.

CHILD ONE : Oh gosh!

[*ENTER* ST GEORGE.]

ST GEORGE : [RUSHING IN.] Curator's on his/her way back ..... hope I haven't been too long. Thanks for holding the f ..... Hey! Where is he/she?

MAIDEN : Well – oh dear.

DRAGON : Bit of a crisis, I'm afraid.

ST GEORGE : Where's my armour?

MAIDEN : In the Curator's cupboard.

ST GEORGE : Well, how the heck .....

CHILD ONE : [SNIFFS.] We don't know what to do.

MAIDEN : The other child's locked in there, too.

ST GEORGE : Well, they'll be reopening this gallery any minute now. I can't be in the picture without my armour.

DRAGON : You might not have a choice.

[<u>SOUNDS</u> OFF-STAGE OF CURATOR RETURNING.]

MAIDEN : Here. Give me that quickly. [SNATCHING GOWN OFF CHILD ONE.] Out you go. [PUSHING CHILD ONE OUT OF PICTURE. CHILD ONE HASTILY SLITHERS ACROSS FLOOR AND ONTO CHAIR. MAIDEN REARRANGES HERSELF AND ST GEORGE JUMPS BACK INTO

THE ART GALLERY

                      PLACE WITHOUT ARMOUR. DRAGON IS HOLDING LANCE.]

                      [*ENTER* CURATOR.]

CURATOR : [LOOKING HARD AT CHILD ONE.] Now, just where have you been? I hope you haven't been up to anything you shouldn't, young lady/young man.

CHILD ONE : No, no I'm getting on with my drawing.

CURATOR : Well you'll have to move in a moment, because this gallery opens again .... [LOOKING AT WATCH.] ..... in precisely one minute and fifty-five seconds. Pack up your things and I'll take that chair. [HE DOES SO AND WALKS TOWARDS THE CUPBOARD.]

ST GEORGE : [TO CHILD ONE.] Distract him as soon as he unlocks the cupboard and I'll grab your friend and my armour. Now ..... when I say "go" .....

                      [CURATOR UNLOCKS AND OPENS CUPBOARD TO PUT CHAIR IN.]

ST GEORGE : "Go".

                      [CURATOR PUTS CHAIR IN BUT BEFORE HE/SHE CAN LOCK IT AGAIN CHILD ONE RUSHES UP AND STARTS TALKING TO HIM/HER.]

CHILD ONE : Excuse me, do you know about Narcissus?

CURATOR : Well, what do you want to know.

THE ART GALLERY

CHILD ONE : About the painting ..... and ..... um ..... who he was ..... and ... um .....

[ST GEORGE CREEPS UP AND GRABS CHILD TWO AS CURATOR LAUNCHES INTO SPIEL ABOUT NARCISSUS.]

CURATOR: Well now miss, ... [MECHANICALLY.] Legend has it that Narcissus, a beautiful youth, rejected the love of the nymph Echo, and as a punishment was made to fall in love with his own reflection in a stream. He pined away for love of himself and in the exact spot where he died there sprang up a flower which was then named after him.

[CHILD ONE THEN ENGAGES CURATOR IN A SILENT MIMED CONVERSATION.]

ST GEORGE : [TO CHILD TWO.] – Where's my armour?

CHILD TWO : I took it off – it was rather hot – uncomfortable ..... I think it was too big for me.

ST GEORGE : By Jupiter ..... you don't make things easy do you?

CHILD TWO : Sorry, I think it's just inside the door.

ST GEORGE : [RUSHING BACK TO PICTURE.]. Wait there!

[ST GEORGE GRABS LANCE FROM DRAGON AND SNEAKS BACK TO THE CUPBOARD – WATCHED OUT OF CORNER OF CHILD ONE'S EYE AS SHE KEEPS CURATOR CHATTING. ST GEORGE TAKES LANCE AND HOOKS IT ONTO

THE ART GALLERY

[ARMOUR – DRAWS IT OUT OF CUPBOARD AND HEADS BACK TO THE PAINTING. ST GEORGE STEPS INTO PAINTING – MAIDEN HANDS HER LILY TO DRAGON AND STARTS HELPING GEORGE ON WITH HIS ARMOUR – GEORGE PASSES LANCE TO DRAGON. CHILD TWO MOVES UP TO THE PAINTING.]

CURATOR : Well, I must be getting on.

[CURATOR WALKS TOWARDS THE PICTURE AS CHILD ONE LOOKS HORRIFIED. DRAGON KEEPS HOLD OF LILY BUT DROPS LANCE WHICH CHILD TWO CATCHES.]

NOTE: "PICTURE" IS MORE OR LESS BACK IN PLACE - APART FROM MISSING LANCE AND LILY IN THE WRONG HANDS.

CURATOR : [TO CHILD TWO.] Here! you young scoundrel. What are you doing with that lance? Give it to me at once.

CHILD TWO : It's not yours – it doesn't belong to you.

CURATOR : Don't you be cheeky.

[CHILD TWO STRUGGLES WITH CURATOR OVER LANCE PULLS AWAY WITH IT AND RUNS OFF, DODGES ROUND CHILD ONE, RUNS BACK TO PICTURE CHASED BY CURATOR AND HANDS LANCE IN TO ST GEORGE. CHILD TWO RUNS BACK TO CHILD ONE AND THEY BOTH FLEE THE GALLERY TOGETHER.]

CURATOR : Young hooligans ..... I've a good mind to .....

[CURATOR EXAMINES PICTURE FRAME FOR DUST WITH FINGER, LOOKS PUZZLED AS

THE ART GALLERY

HE/SHE STARES AT THE PAINTING – DRAGON IS STILL HOLDING MAIDEN'S LILY – HE/SHE TURNS AWAY AND SCRATCHES HIS/HER HEAD – GOES BACK LOOKS AGAIN. THEN CROSSES OVER TO LOCK CUPBOARD – DURING WHICH TIME DRAGON HANDS LILY BACK TO MAIDEN. CHARACTERS IN PICTURE ALL LOOK RELIEVED AND FREEZE AS CURATOR LOOKS BACK – TAKES GLASSES OFF – CLEANS THEM – PUTS THEM BACK ON – CHECKS FOR THE LAST TIME AND SMILES.]

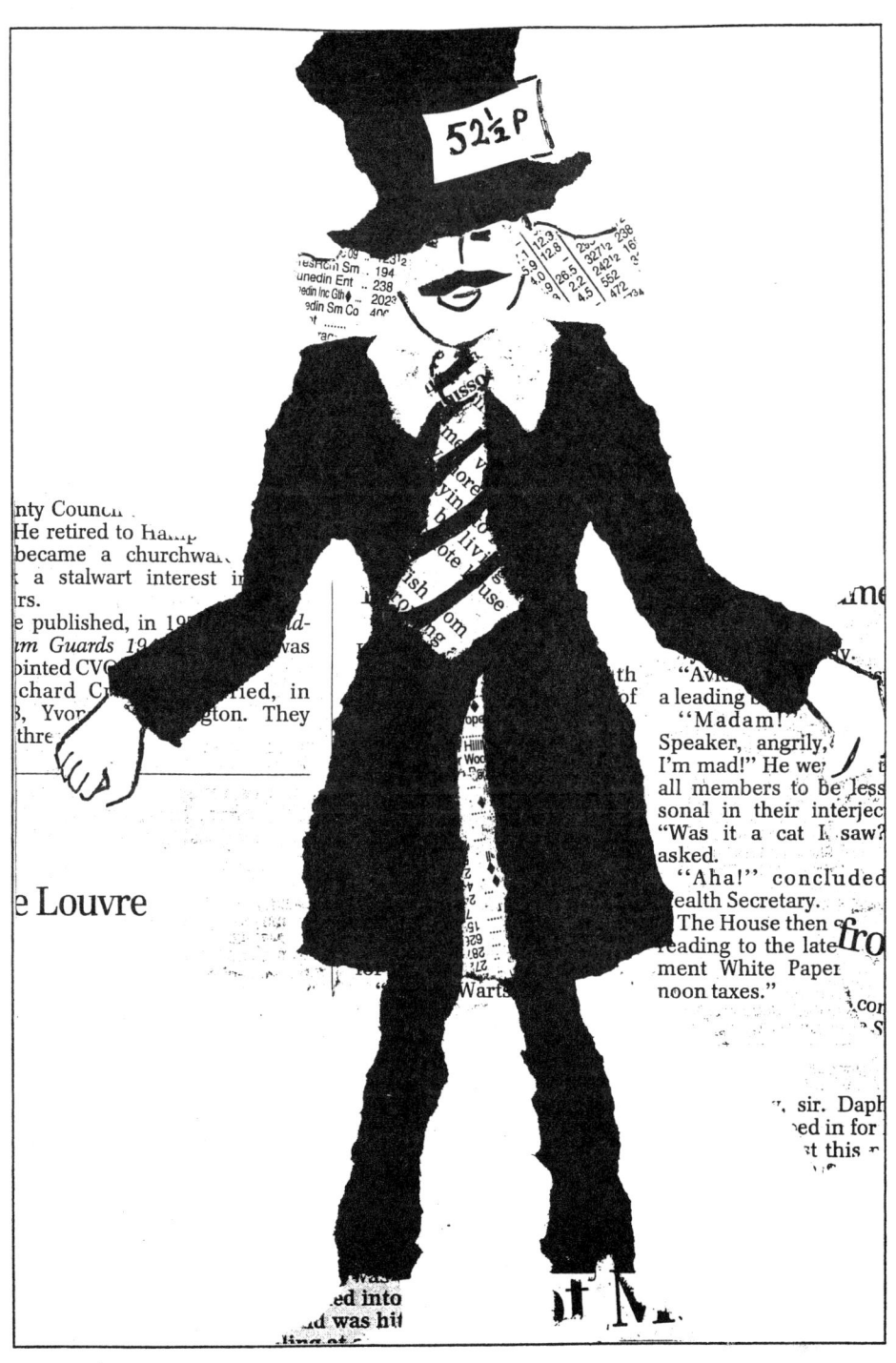

Alice in the Wild Wood

10. Alice In The Wild Wood

AN EXTRACT FROM THE PLAY

NO OF PLAYERS : 6 • 7 • 8 • 9 • 10

CHARACTERS :   ALICE *
                    RABBIT
                    RED QUEEN
                    DORMOUSE
                    TWEEDLE A
                    TWEEDLE B
                    CHESHIRE CAT
                    MAD HATTER
                    CATERPILLAR
                    MOTHER NATURE *

                                  * DO NOT DOUBLE

NOTE :   RABBIT} MAY DOUBLE WITH DORMOUSE **
           TWEEDLE A} MAY DOUBLE WITH MAD HATTER
           TWEEDLE B} MAY DOUBLE WITH CATERPILLAR
           QUEEN} MAY DOUBLE WITH CAT

      ** IF DOUBLING DORMOUSE SIMPLY SWITCHES HEAD-DRESSES AS HIS HEAD APPEARS OUT OF THE TEAPOT BUT BODY IS NEVER SEEN.

PROPS/COSTUMES :   OVERSIZE TEAPOT
                          RABBIT HEAD-DRESS/MASK
                          DORMOUSE HEAD-DRESS/MASK
                          CAT HEAD-DRESS/MASK
                          CATERPILLAR HEAD-DRESS/MASK
                          POCKET WATCH
                          WHITE 'KID' GLOVES
                          HATTER'S HAT

ALICE IN THE WILD WOOD

SOUND : DOOR BELL/HAND BELL *

* EITHER ONE

NOTE : THE STAGE IS DIVIDED INTO 2 AREAS. TO ONE SIDE IS A WOOD AND TO THE OTHER A PICNIC SPOT WITH A CHEQUERED TABLECLOTH AND AN OVERSIZED TEAPOT FROM WHICH THE DORMOUSE EMERGES FROM TIME TO TIME.

SCENE ONE : THE WOOD. ALICE IS DOZING ON THE GROUND. TWEEDLE A AND TWEEDLE B ARE LOOKING AT HER WITH CURIOSITY.

    ALICE • WHITE RABBIT • TWEEDLE A • TWEEDLE B • RED QUEEN • CHESHIRE CAT

[*ENTER* WHITE RABBIT CARRYING PAIR OF GLOVES, RUNNING AND MUTTERING TO HIMSELF.

RABBIT :   [LOOKING AT WATCH.] I'm late, I'm late.

    [TWEEDLE A AND TWEEDLE B MELT AWAY.]

ALICE :   Come back please, ...

TWEEDLE A :⎤
TWEEDLE B :⎦ He's late, he's late, ...

    [TWEEDLE A AND TWEEDLE B *EXIT.* CHORUS OFF-STAGE.] He's late, he's late, he's late . . . . .

    [*EXIT* RABBIT. *ENTER* QUEEN 'APPEARING FROM NOWHERE'.]

ALICE :   I've lost my way.

136

QUEEN : I'm sure I don't know what you mean by 'your' way. All the ways round here belong to me.

ALICE : I am sorry. I didn't think . . . . .

QUEEN : You should not speak without thinking.

[*ENTER* TWEEDLE A.]

TWEEDLE A : Or think without speaking.

ALICE : Is that the same thing?

[*ENTER* TWEEDLE B.]

TWEEDLE B : Not on Thursdays.

ALICE : Oh! There are two of you.

TWEEDLE A : We're brothers.

ALICE : I see.

TWEEDLE B : No A and B.

TWEEDLE A : Tweedle A and Tweedle B.

TWEEDLE B : Are you Tweedle C?

ALICE : I'm Alice.

TWEEDLE B : I could have sworn you said you were C.

ALICE : I'm Alice.

QUEEN : No swearing allowed here. Where have you come from, little girl?

ALICE IN THE WILD WOOD

ALICE :   I'm not sure.

TWEEDLE A :   The seashore?

ALICE :   No, [POINTING.] from over there.

QUEEN :   Oh, you mean Thursday.

ALICE :   I can't remember which day I started.

QUEEN :   Well I can't imagine how you expect to get anywhere if you don't know where you've come from. Have you seen the white rabbit?

ALICE :   Yes I have. I followed him here, then he rushed off and I lost my way.

QUEEN :   <u>My</u> way.

ALICE :   I didn't mean . . . . .

QUEEN :   You don't think, you don't mean. You seem to be a very ignorant sort of a girl.

ALICE :   I didn't used to be. Everything's so different here.

QUEEN :   You can't stay here unless you improve your mind. Boys, you'd better take Alice to school.

TWEEDLE A :
TWEEDLE B :   Which school, Your Majesty?

QUEEN :   Let me see. She could go to the School of Porpoises to learn reading and writing . . . . . or maybe Art School to learn Drawing and Painting and Mystery, ancient and modern. But on second thoughts, perhaps you'd better take her back to Tuesday so she can choose herself.

TWEEDLE A :⎱
TWEEDLE B :⎰   Yes, Your Majesty.

[TWEEDLE A AND TWEEDLE B *EXIT*. ALICE *EXITS*. BETWEEN THEM.]

QUEEN :   I don't know what things are coming to, or where they are going, for that matter. And my rabbit is late again.

[*ENTER*. RABBIT.]

RABBIT :   Did someone call?

QUEEN :   Oh, there you are. Where have you been?

RABBIT :   I'm sorry Your M-majesty. I've been dealing with your pack of cards and the Jack has gone missing again.

QUEEN :   Very careless!

RABBIT :   But the Cheshire Cat is hunting for him.

QUEEN :   Which day did he go?

RABBIT :   Wednesday I think, Your Majesty.

QUEEN :   Less thinking and more looking please.

[QUEEN *EXITS*.]

ALICE IN THE WILD WOOD

RABBIT: Y . . . . . yes, Your M-majesty.

[RABBIT *EXITS.*]

CAT: [FROM OFF-STAGE.] What are <u>you</u> doing here?

[ALICE *ENTERS* FROM OPPOSITE SIDE AND LOOKS HIGH AND LOW FOR THE CAT. CHESHIRE CAT *ENTERS.* GRINNING.]

ALICE: Oh, it's the Cheshire Cat. Chess Catkins would you tell me please where I ought to go from here.

CAT: That depends a good deal on where you want to go.

ALICE: The Tweedles mentioned something about a picnic.

CAT: Ah, that would be the Mad Hatter's picnic.

ALICE: I don't want to go among mad people.

CAT: We're all mad around here. So are you.

ALICE: How do you know I'm mad?

CAT: You must be, or you wouldn't have come here.

ALICE: I'm getting very hungry.

CAT: Let me help you to find the picnic. Follow me.

[CAT LEADS THE WAY AND ALICE FOLLOWS THEY WEAVE AROUND WOOD AND *EXIT.*]

ALICE IN THE WILD WOOD

SCENE TWO : A PICNIC. MAD HATTER AND CATERPILLAR ARE SEATED.

ALICE • HATTER • CATERPILLAR •
MOTHER NATURE • DORMOUSE • RABBIT •
RED QUEEN • CHESHIRE CAT

[*ENTER* ALICE.]

HATTER : [AS ALICE APPEARS.] No room! No room! No room!

CATERPILLAR : No room! No room! No room!

ALICE : There's plenty of room. [SITS DOWN.]

CATERPILLAR : Have some wine.

ALICE : I don't see any wine.

CATERPILLAR : There isn't any.

ALICE : Then it wasn't very polite of you to offer it.

HATTER : It wasn't very polite of you to sit down without being invited.

ALICE : [TO HATTER.] Is it your picnic?

[MOTHER NATURE *ENTERS.*]

MOTHER N : As a matter of fact, it is my picnic. And you may sit down, or sit up if you prefer.

HATTER : May, June or July.

MOTHER N : Caterpillar, would you please wake the Dormouse.

ALICE IN THE WILD WOOD

CATERPILLAR :	He's only been asleep since Tuesday.
MOTHER N :	I wonder if he's learnt his poem yet?
HATTER :	Was he learning a new poem?
MOTHER N :	'Twinkle, Twinkle'.
ALICE :	I think I know that one.
HATTER :	Everyone knows it, of course.
ALICE :	Twinkle, twinkle little star,
HATTER :	No! No! No! Completely wrong.
CATERPILLAR :	Absolutely wrong.
MOTHER :	Where do you go to school dear?
ALICE :	Well, yesterday I went with Tweedle A and Tweedle B.
MOTHER N :	Well! they're not very bright.
HATTER :	No, they don't twinkle at all.
CATERPILLAR :	<u>Bat</u>. [VERY LOUDLY.]
ALICE :	I beg your pardon?
CATERPILLAR :	Twinkle, twinkle little bat!
HATTER :	How I wonder what you're at! Up above the world you fly, Like a tea-tray in the sky. ..... Twinkle, twinkle .....

ALICE IN THE WILD WOOD

DORMOUSE : [EMERGING FROM TEAPOT SLEEPILY.]
Twinkle, twinkle, twinkle, twinkle, twinkle.

MOTHER N : Someone pinch that Dormouse.

DORMOUSE : I wasn't asleep. I heard every word you said.

MOTHER N : [DORMOUSE FALLS ASLEEP.] Have a lettuce sandwich.

[DORMOUSE SLIDES BACK INSIDE TEAPOT.]

HATTER : The Caterpillar has eaten them all.

CATERPILLAR : It was the Dormouse.

HATTER : That is typical, absolutely typical – always blaming everyone else – and where's the sugar?

CATERPILLAR : Don't look at me.

HATTER : At whom should I look then?

CATERPILLAR : Look at Alice.

MOTHER N : Have you seen the sugar dear?

ALICE : I'm afraid not.

MOTHER N : No need to be afraid unless the Red Queen's about. She suspects everyone of stealing her sugar ..... and her jam tarts.

ALICE : Oh dear.

HATTER : Everyone knows it was the Jack.

ALICE IN THE WILD WOOD

MOTHER N : [SIGHING.] Well, we shall just have to dig for more sugar.

ALICE : [WIDE-EYED.] Is there a sugar mine?

MOTHER N : No, it isn't yours – it isn't really even ours. Everything here belongs to the Red Queen, but she lets us have some on Tuesdays and Fridays.

CATERPILLAR : It's the Dormouse's turn to dig.

HATTER : He's asleep again.

ALICE : He does seem to sleep a lot.

[HATTER TAPS ON TEAPOT.]

DORMOUSE : [POPS UP AND YAWNS.] You tapped? [SLEEPILY RUBS EYES.]

HATTER : You napped.

CATERPILLAR : Again.

DORMOUSE : [NOTICING ALICE.] Who's this?

MOTHER N : This is Alice.

DORMOUSE : Where did she come from?

CATERPILLAR : She doesn't know.

DORMOUSE : Oh. [NODS OFF AGAIN AND SLIDES DOWN OUT OF SIGHT.]

MOTHER N : Well, well. Time to move, I think.

ALICE : Where to?

MOTHER N : Saturday, of course.

HATTER : First course Friday, middle course Saturday......

CATERPILLAR : ..... Pudding on Sunday.

MOTHER N : Someone ring the bell, please.

[HATTER MIMES IT. SOUND OF BELL RINGING AND RABBIT *ENTERS*. APPEARING BY MAGIC.]

RABBIT : You rang, my lady?

MOTHER N : I did indeed. Where have you been all this time?

RABBIT : I'm so sorry I'm late. I lost my gloves again.

CATERPILLAR : [SARCASTICALLY.] That makes a change.

MOTHER N : Did you bring the book?

RABBIT : The b-book?

MOTHER N : The story book.

RABBIT : [SHAKES HEAD.] Oh dear, dear me ..... [WALKING BACKWARDS.] ..... er ..... er ..... [*EXITS*]

MOTHER N : We'd better wake the Dormouse.

HATTER : He hasn't had his full complement of sleep yet.

ALICE : What is a full complement?

ALICE IN THE WILD WOOD

HATTER : In his case about a month I think.

ALICE : Good gracious.

CATERPILLAR : Well, are we having a story or what?

DORMOUSE : [WAKING UP.] Is it time for a story yet?

CATERPILLAR : Ah! You've decided to join us have you?

HATTER : [POINTING OUT ALICE.] Does she know any stories?

ALICE : I think I know a story.

CATERPILLAR : You didn't know 'Twinkle, Twinkle'.

DORMOUSE : Twinkle, twinkle, twinkle ..... twinkle ..... twinkle ..... [FALLS ASLEEP. SNORES.]

HATTER : Well, we all know the story about the Walrus .....

CATERPILLAR : ..... and the Carpenter.

[*ENTER* QUEEN WHO SAILS IN REGALLY FOLLOWED A MOMENT LATER BY BREATHLESS RABBIT WHO IS TRYING TO CATCH UP.]

QUEEN :
HATTER :   } The time has come, ...
CATERPILLAR :

[RABBIT IS DESPERATELY TRYING TO CATCH HIS BREATH.]

QUEEN : The Walrus said, ...

QUEEN :
HATTER :   } To talk of many things:
CATERPILLAR :

ALL :   Of shoes- and ships – and sealing-wax -
                Of cabbages – and kings –
                And why the sea is boiling hot –
                And whether pigs have wings.

                [RABBIT REGAINS COMPOSURE, SMARTENS HIMSELF UP, ETC.]

ALICE :
RABBIT :   } But wait a bit,
MOTHER N :

ALICE :
RABBIT :   } The Oysters cried,
MOTHER N :

ALICE :
RABBIT :   } Before we have our chat;
MOTHER N :

ALICE :
RABBIT :   } For some of us are out of breath,
MOTHER N :

ALICE :
RABBIT :   } And all of us are fat!
MOTHER N :

QUEEN :
HATTER :   } No hurry!
CATERPILLAR :

HATTER :   Said the Carpenter.

ALL :   They thanked him much for that.

ALICE IN THE WILD WOOD

QUEEN :
HATTER : } A loaf of bread,
CATERPILLAR :

HATTER : The Walrus said,

QUEEN :
HATTER : } Is what we chiefly need:
CATERPILLAR :

QUEEN :
HATTER : } Pepper and vinegar besides
CATERPILLAR :

QUEEN :
HATTER : Are very good indeed –
CATERPILLAR :

QUEEN :
HATTER : } Now if you're ready, Oysters dear,
CATERPILLAR :

QUEEN :
HATTER : } We can begin to feed.
CATERPILLAR :

ALICE :
RABBIT : } But not on us!
MOTHER N:

ALICE :
RABBIT : } The Oysters cried,
MOTHER N:

ALICE :
RABBIT : } Turning a little blue.
MOTHER N:

ALICE: RABBIT: MOTHER N:	After such kindness, that would be
ALICE: RABBIT: MOTHER N:	A dismal thing to do!
QUEEN: HATTER: CATERPILLAR	The night is fine,
CATERPILLAR:	The Walrus said.
HATTER:	Do you admire the view?
QUEEN: HATTER:	It was so kind of you to come!
QUEEN: HATTER:	And you are very nice!
CATERPILLAR:	The Carpenter said nothing but Cut us another slice. I wish you were not quite so deaf – I've had to ask you twice!
QUEEN: HATTER:	It seems a shame,
QUEEN: HATTER:	The Walrus said,
QUEEN: HATTER:	To play them such a trick,
QUEEN: HATTER:	After we've brought them out so far,
QUEEN: HATTER:	And made them trot so quick!

ALICE IN THE WILD WOOD

CATERPILLAR : The Carpenter said nothing but
'The butter's spread too thick!'

QUEEN : I weep for you,

HATTER : The Walrus said :

QUEEN :
HATTER : } I deeply sympathize.
CATERPILLAR :

ALL : With sobs and tears he sorted out
Those of the largest size,
Holding his pocket-handkerchief
Before his streaming eyes.

QUEEN :
HATTER : } O Oysters –
CATERPILLAR :

HATTER : Said the Carpenter,

QUEEN :
HATTER : } You've had a pleasant run!
CATERPILLAR :

QUEEN :
HATTER : } Shall we be trotting home again?'
CATERPILLAR :

[*EXIT* QUEEN FOLLOWED BY RABBIT.]

ALL : But answer came there none –
And this was scarcely odd, because
They'd eaten every one.

NOTE : LINES OF THIS POEM MAY BE
SHARED DIFFERENTLY TO SUIT
VOICES.

ALICE IN THE WILD WOOD

ALICE : How awfully, awfully sad.

ALL : Yes isn't it.

[ALICE, HATTER, CATERPILLAR AND MOTHER NATURE FORM A CIRCLE AND WEEP IN TURN AROUND THE CIRCLE UNTIL CAT *ENTERS*.]

CAT : Goodness gracious is that the time?

ALICE : Is what the time?

CATERPILLAR : Time for tea.

HATTER : You've had tea.

CATERPILLAR : It seems a long time ago.

ALICE : I didn't have any tea.

HATTER : You should have been faster.

[DORMOUSE WAKES.]

DORMOUSE : You have to be very, very fast if you want a lettuce sandwich ..... [LOOKING AT CATERPILLAR.] before he's eaten them all.

[DORMOUSE YAWNS AND SINKS DOWN INTO TEAPOT.]

CATERPILLAR : [SPEAKING INTO TEAPOT.] Are you being critical?

DORMOUSE : [PAUSE. REAPPEARS.] I don't know ..... GOES BACK DOWN INTO TEAPOT. <u>SNORING.</u>]

ALICE IN THE WILD WOOD

CAT : [TO CATERPILLAR.] Have you really eaten all the sandwiches?

CATERPILLAR : I may have had one or two.

HATTER : One or two? You've eaten every last plateful.

MOTHER N : The Queen will be furious.

CAT : She's expecting six platefuls by four o'clock.

ALICE : How dreadful. What can we do?

MOTHER N : We shall have to find more lettuces.

ALICE : Where shall we look?

HATTER : I think we should start with Monday.

CAT : Late with the lettuces ..... you will be in trouble.

MOTHER N : We'll harvest more. Everyone must help. Wake the Dormouse again.

CATERPILLAR : Why?

HATTER : To help with the lettuces you silly worm. [SHOUTING INTO TEAPOT.] Wakey, wakey. Rise and shine.

DORMOUSE : [EMERGING.] I wasn't asleep. I heard every word you said. ..... I was just resting my eyes.

CATERPILLAR : A likely tale.

DORMOUSE : Yes it is isn't it.

ALICE : What is?

DORMOUSE : My tail ..... very likeable I think.

CATERPILLAR : Idiot.

[DORMOUSE SINKS INTO TEAPOT.]

HATTER : [SPEAKING INTO TEAPOT.] Now don't take umbrage. [PAUSE. NO RESPONSE. *EXITS.*]

DORMOUSE : [EMERGING.] Haven't taken anything but a small lettuce sandwich all week.
[DOZES OFF AGAIN SINKS OUT OF SIGHT.]

MOTHER N : Alice, can you help, dear?

ALICE : Yes, of course.

MOTHER N : And you, Cheshire Cat?

CAT : Yes, yes, yes indeed. ..... Yes of course.

[MOTHER NATURE POINTS. CAT E*XITS*. HATTER *ENTERS.*]

HATTER : Calamity! Catastrophe! Disaster!

MOTHER N : Whatever's the matter, Hatter?

HATTER : They were there when I tucked them up last night.

[*ENTER* RABBIT.]

RABBIT : Who were?

ALICE IN THE WILD WOOD

HATTER: There when I read them a bedtime story.

ALICE: Who? Who?

HATTER: Rows and rows in their little beds.
[SOBBING.]

CATERPILLAR: Ah ..... um ..... rows of what?

HATTER: Lettuces of course. Gone ..... all gone.

[CATERPILLAR STARTS TO SNEAK OFF.]

MOTHER N: Caterpillar, come here. What do you know about this?

CATERPILLAR: Me?

HATTER: Yes you!

RABBIT: Did you take them all?

CATERPILLAR: Not all. There were plenty left when .....

HATTER: When?

CATERPILLAR: When I borrowed one or two.

MOTHER N: Borrowed?

RABBIT: Borrowed?

HATTER: You know they belong to the Red Queen. She'll be hopping mad.

CATERPILLAR: We're all mad.

HATTER: So we are.

ALICE IN THE WILD WOOD

QUEEN: [FROM OFF-STAGE.] Where's that White Rabbit?

RABBIT: Oh goodness gracious. Oh dear! Oh dear!

[QUEEN *ENTERS.*]

QUEEN: Where are my lettuce sandwiches? [TO ALICE.] Have you seen them child?

ALICE: No, Your Majesty.

QUEEN: What happens when I don't get my sandwiches?

RABBIT: You get very angry, ma'am.

CATERPILLAR: Terribly cross, ma'am.

HATTER: Absolutely mad, ma'am.

CATERPILLAR: Very, very hungry, Your Majesty.

MOTHER N: Tired out, Your Majesty.

QUEEN: Exactly. So look lively Alice, you're in charge!

MOTHER N: [TO ALICE.] You're in charge dear.

[ALL CHARACTERS IN TURN SPIN ALICE AROUND SAYING "YOU'RE IN CHARGE" BEFORE *EXITING* AND CONTINUING TO SHOUT "YOU'RE IN CHARGE" FROM OFF-STAGE. THE QUEEN POINTS AN ACCUSING FINGER AT ALICE WHO PUTS HER HANDS OVER HER EARS AND SINKS TO THE GROUND. QUEEN SWEEPS OFF, *EXITS.* RABBIT *ENTERS,* CREEPING SILENTLY, HELPS ALICE TO HER FEET. OTHER PLAYERS *RE-ENTER* – ALL BOW.]

ADDITIONAL TITLES AVAILABLE

All books may be ordered direct from:

DRAMATIC LINES   PO BOX 201   TWICKENHAM   TW2 5RQ   ENGLAND

freefone: 0800 5429570
fax: 020 8296 9503
www.dramaticlines.co.uk

MONOLOGUES

THE SIEVE
AND OTHER SCENES
Heather Stephens
ISBN 0 9522224 0 X

The Sieve contains unusual short original monologues valid for junior acting examinations. The material in The Sieve has proved popular with winning entries worldwide in drama festival competitions. Although these monologues were originally written for the 8-14 year age range they have been used by adult actors for audition and performance pieces. Each monologue is seen through the eyes of a young person with varied subject matter including tough social issues such as fear, 'Television Spinechiller', senile dementia, 'Seen Through a Glass Darkly' and withdrawal from the world in 'The Sieve'. Other pieces include: 'A Game of Chicken', 'The Present', 'Balloon Race' and a widely used new adaptation of Hans Christian Andersen's 'The Little Match Girl' in monologue form.

CABBAGE
AND OTHER SCENES
Heather Stephens
ISBN 0 9522224 5 0

Following the success of The Sieve, Heather Stephens has written an additional book of monologues with thought provoking and layered subject matter valid for junior acting examinations. The Cabbage monologues were originally written for the 8-14 year age range but have been used by adult actors for audition and performance pieces. The Aberfan slag heap disaster issues are graphically confronted in 'Aberfan Prophecy' and 'The Surviving Twin' whilst humorous perceptions of life are observed by young people in 'The Tap Dancer' and 'Cabbage'. Other pieces include: 'The Dinner Party Guest', 'Nine Lives' and a new adaptation of Robert Browning's 'The Pied Piper' seen through the eyes of the crippled child.

ALONE IN MY ROOM Ken Pickering
ORIGINAL MONOLOGUES ISBN 0 9537770 0 6

This collection of short original monologues includes extracts from the author's longer works in addition to the classics. Provocative issues such as poverty and land abuse are explored in 'One Child at a Time', 'The Young Person Talks' and 'Turtle Island' with adaptations from 'Jane Eyre', Gulliver's Travels' and 'Oliver Twist' and well loved authors include Dostoyevsky. These monologues have a wide variety of applications including syllabus recommendation for various acting examinations. Each monologue has a brief background description and acting notes.

DUOLOGUES

PEARS Heather Stephens
  ISBN 0 9522224 6 9

These thought provoking and unusual short original duologues provide new material for speech and drama festival candidates in the 8-14 year age range. The scenes have also been widely used for junior acting examinations and in a variety of school situations and theatrical applications. Challenging topics in Pears include the emotive issues of child migration, 'Blondie', 'The Outback Institution' and bullying 'Bullies', other scenes examine friendship, 'The Best of Friends', 'The Row' and envy, 'Never the Bridesmaid'. New adaptations of part scenes from 'Peace' by Aristophanes and 'Oliver Twist' by Charles Dickens are also included.

TOGETHER NOW Ken Pickering
ORIGINAL DUOLOGUES ISBN 0 9537770 1 4

This collection of short duologues includes extracts from Ken Pickering's longer works together with new original pieces. The variety of experiences explored in the scenes can all be easily identified with, such as an awkward situation, 'You Tell Her', and the journey of self knowledge in 'Gilgamesh', whilst 'Mobile phones', 'Sales' and 'Food' observe realistic situations in an interesting and perceptive way. Other duologues based on well known stories include 'Snow White' and 'The Pilgrim's Progress'. Each piece has a brief background description and acting notes. The scenes have syllabus recommendation for a number of examination boards and wide variety of theatrical and school applications.

MONOLOGUES AND DUOLOGUES

SHAKESPEARE THE REWRITES
Claire Jones
ISBN 0 9522224 8 5

A collection of short monologues and duologues for female players. The scenes are from rewrites of Shakespeare plays from 1670 to the present day written by authors seeking to embellish original texts for performances, to add prequels or sequels or satisfy their own very personal ideas about production. This material is fresh and unusual and will provide exciting new audition and examination material. Comparisons with the original Shakespeare text are fascinating and this book will provide a useful contribution to Theatre Study work from GCSE to beyond 'A' level. Contributors include James Thurber (Macbeth) Arnold Wesker (Merchant of Venice) and Peter Ustinov (Romanoff and Juliet). The collection also includes a most unusual Japanese version of Hamlet.

RESOURCES

DRAMA LESSONS IN ACTION
Antoinette Line
ISBN 0 9522224 2 6

Resource material suitable for classroom and assembly use for teachers of junior and secondary age pupils. Lessons are taught through improvisation, these are not presented as 'model lessons' but provide ideas for adaptation and further development. Lessons include warm-up and speech exercises and many themes are developed through feelings such as timidity, resentfulness, sensitivity and suspicion. Material can be used by groups of varying sizes and pupils are asked to respond to texts from a diverse selection of well known authors including: Roald Dahl, Ogden Nash, John Betjeman, Ted Hughes, Michael Rosen, and Oscar Wilde.

AAARGH TO ZIZZ
135 DRAMA GAMES
Graeme Talboys
ISBN 0 9537770 5 7

This valuable resource material has been created by a drama teacher and used mostly in formal drama lessons but also in informal situations such as clubs and parties. The games are extremely flexible, from warm up to cool down, inspiration to conclusion and from deadly serious to purest fun and the wide variety ranges from laughing and rhythm activities to building a sentence and word association. Many games could be used as part of a PSHE programme together with activities connected with 'fair play'. The games are easily adapted and each has notes on setting up details of straightforward resources needed. All this material has been

DRAMA•DANCE•SINGING
TEACHER RESOURCE BOOK

edited by John Nicholas
ISBN 0 9537770 2 2

This collection of drama, dance and singing lesson activities has been drawn from a bank of ideas used by the Stagecoach Theatre Arts Schools teachers. Clearly presented lessons include speech and drama exercises, games and improvisations often developed as a response to emotions. Dance activities include warm-ups, basic dance positions, improvisations, versatile dance exercises and routines while singing activities help to develop rhythm and notation as well as providing enjoyable games to develop the voice. Activities can be easily adapted for large or small group use and are suitable for 6 - 16 year olds in a fun yet challenging way.

MUSICAL PLAYS

THREE CHEERS FOR MRS BUTLER adapted by Vicky Ireland
ISBN 0 9537770 4 9

This versatile musical play about everyday school life is for anyone who has ever been to school. It features the poems and characters created by Allan Ahlberg with a foreword by Michael Rosen, songs by Colin Matthews and Steven Markwick and was first performed at the Polka Theatre for Children, London. The two acts of 40 minutes each can be performed by children, adults or a mixture of both and the play can be produced with a minimum cast of 7 or a large cast of any size, with or without music and songs, as well as having a wide variety of other musical and dramatic applications.

INTRODUCING OSCAR
The Selfish Giant & The Happy Prince

Veronica Bennetts
ISBN 0 9537770 3 0

Oscar Wilde's timeless stories for children have been chosen for adaptation because of the rich opportunities offered for imaginative exploration and the capacity to vividly illuminate many aspects of the human condition. The original dialogue, lyrics and music by Veronica Bennetts can be adapted and modified according to the needs of the pupils and individual schools or drama groups. The Selfish Giant runs for 25 minutes and The Happy Prince for 1 hour 15 minutes. Both musical can be used for Trinity College, *London.* examinations and are ideal for end of term productions, for drama groups and primary and secondary schools.

TEENAGE PLAYS

WHAT IS THE MATTER WITH MARY JANE?   Wendy Harmer
ISBN 0 9522224 4 2

This monodrama about a recovering anorexic and bulimic takes the audience into the painful reality of a young woman afflicted by eating disorders. The play is based on the personal experience of actress Sancia Robinson and has proved hugely popular in Australia. It is written with warmth and extraordinary honesty and the language, humour and style appeal to current youth culture. A study guide for teachers and students is included in this English edition ensuring that the material is ideal for use in the secondary school classroom and for PSHE studies, drama departments in schools and colleges in addition to amateur and professional performance.

X-STACY   Margery Forde
ISBN 0 9522224 9 3

Margery Forde's powerful play centres on the rave culture and illicit teenage drug use and asks tough questions about family, friends and mutual responsibilities. The play has proved hugely successful in Australia and this English edition is published with extensive teachers' notes by Helen Radian, Lecturer of Drama at Queensland University of Technology, to enrich its value for the secondary school classroom, PSHE studies, English and drama departments.

ONE ACT PLAYS

WILL SHAKESPEARE SAVE US!   Paul Nimmo
WILL SHAKESPEARE SAVE THE KING! ISBN 0 9522224 1 8

Two versatile plays in which famous speeches and scenes from Shakespeare are acted out as part of a comic story about a bored king and his troupe of players. These plays are suitable for the 11-18 year age range and have been produced with varying ages within the same cast and also performed by adults to a young audience. The plays can be produced as a double bill, alternatively each will stand on its own, performed by a minimum cast of 10 without a set, few props and modern dress or large cast, traditional set and costumes. The scripts are ideal for reading aloud by classes or groups and provide an excellent introduction to the works of Shakespeare. Both plays have been successfully performed on tour and at the Shakespeare's Globe in London.

SUGAR ON SUNDAYS
AND OTHER PLAYS

Andrew Gordon
ISBN 0 9522224 3 4

A collection of six one act plays bringing history alive through drama. History is viewed through the eyes of ordinary people and each play is packed with details about everyday life, important events and developments of the period. The plays can be used as classroom drama, for school performances and group acting examinations and also as shared texts for the literacy hour. The plays are suitable for children from Key Stage 2 upwards and are 40-50 minutes in length and explore Ancient Egypt, Ancient Greece, Anglo-Saxon and Viking Times, Victorian Britain and the Second World War. A glossary of key words helps to develop children's historical understanding of National Curriculum History Topics and the plays provide opportunities for children to enjoy role play and performance.

TEENAGE SCENES

JELLY BEANS

Joseph McNair Stover
ISBN 0 9522224 7 7

The distinctive style and deceptively simple logic of American writer Joseph McNair Stover has universal appeal with **scenes** that vary in tone from whimsical to serious and focus on young peoples relationships in the contemporary world. The 10 to 15 minute original scenes for 2,3, and 4 players are suitable for 11 year old students through to adult. Minimal use of sets and props makes Jelly Beans ideal for group acting examinations, classroom drama, assemblies, and a wide variety of additional theatrical applications.

ASSEMBLIES

ASSEMBLIES! ASSEMBLIES! ASSEMBLIES!

Kryssy Hurley
ISBN 0 9537770 6 5

These teacher-led assemblies require minimum preparation and have been written by a practising teacher to involve small or large groups. Each assembly lasts 15-20 minutes and is suitable for Key Stages 2 and 3. There are 12 for each term and these explore many PSHE and Citizenship issues including bullying, racism, friendship, co-operation, feeling positive, making responsible choices and decisions, school rules and laws outside school. All have the following sections: *Resource and Organisation, What To Do, Reflection Time and Additional Resources and Activities.*

DRAMATIC LINES HANDBOOKS

SHAKESPEARE FOR AUDITIONS AND EXAMINATIONS

Frank Barrie

SPEECH AND DRAMA

Ann Jones and Bob Cheeseman

THINKING ABOUT PLAYS

Giles Auckland-Lewis and Ken Pickering

PREPARING FOR YOUR DIPLOMA IN DRAMA AND SPEECH

Ken Pickering and Kirsty Findlay

MUSICAL THEATRE

Gerry Tebbutt

EFFECTIVE COMMUNICATION

John Caputo, Jo Palosaari and Ken Pickering